SCRATCHING
THE BEAT SURFACE

Michael McClure

North Point Press
San Francisco
1982

The author wishes to extend his gratitude to the following authors and publishers for their permission to reprint materials included in this volume:
"Peyote Poem," "Point Lobos: Animism," "Night Words: The Ravishing," "Poem," and "For the Death of 100 Whales," from *Hymns to St. Geryon and Dark Brown* by Michael McClure, © 1980 by Michael McClure, reprinted by permission of Grey Fox Press.
"Howl" from *Howl and Other Poems* by Allen Ginsberg, © 1966 by Allen Ginsberg, reprinted by permission of the author and City Light Publishers.
"A Berry Feast" from *The Back Country* by Gary Snyder, © 1957 by Gary Snyder and "Mother Earth: Her Whales" from *Turtle Island* by Gary Snyder, © 1972 by Gary Snyder; "Desultory Days" from *Later* by Robert Creeley, © 1979 by Robert Creeley; and "The Kingfishers" from *Selected Writings* by Charles Olson, © 1966 by Charles Olson are all reprinted by the permission of New Directions Publishing Corporation.
"Plus Ça Change" from *On Bear's Head* by Philip Whalen, © 1969 by Philip Whalen, reprinted by permission of the author.
"The Search" from *Early Selected y Mas: Poems 1949–1966* by Paul Blackburn, © 1972 by Paul Blackburn, reprinted with permission of Black Sparrow Press.
Selections from *Mexico City Blues* by Jack Kerouac, © 1959 by Jack Kerouac, reprinted by permission of Grove Press, Inc.
Untitled poem by Su Tung-p'o to the tune "Immortal by the River," is translated by Wai-lim Yip and appears in his *Chinese Poetry: Major Modes and Genres,* University of California Press, 1976.
Poem by Ontono Yakamochi is from *The Manyōshū: The Nippon Gakujutsu Translation of One Thousand Poems,* Columbia University Press, 1965.
"A Name for All" is from *Complete Poems and Selected Prose* by Hart Crane, edited by Brom Weber, Liveright and Co., 1966.

ACKNOWLEDGMENTS

The essays in Part One, "Scratching the Beat Surface," have been revised from the Gray Lectures delivered by the author at the State University of New York at Buffalo; he and the publisher wish to thank Robert Creeley and Robert Bertholf for their assistance with those lectures.

Portions of these essays have appeared in *Io, Raise the Stakes, Clear Creek,* and the *Journal of Biological Experience.*

The author and publisher especially wish to thank Larry Keenan for his assistance on this book.

CONTENTS

Part One

SCRATCHING
THE BEAT SURFACE

in memoriam Olson

I.

THE BEAT SURFACE

Because it is beautiful! It is beautiful!
From oh oh oh oh over there!
This way! Way! Way! Way! Way!
This way! Bew! Bew! Bew! Beautiful!
Here! Here! Here! Here! — Here!
                    from a hunting song

In 1958 I ate the American Indian drug peyote for the first time. Peyote is, of course, the cactus *Lophophora williamsii* — a small, spineless, flat-topped plant found mainly in the vicinity of Laredo and Northern Sonora. In those days, in San Francisco where I was living with my wife and infant daughter in an apartment high over the city in a building otherwise inhabited by painters, there was a mystery about drugs and they were taken for joy, for consciousness, for spiritual elevation, or for what the Romantic poet Keats called "Soul-making." He expressed it in the phrase, "Call the world if you please the Vale of Soul-making." He believed that we do not necessarily have a soul, but that we have the propensity to create one. Therefore, I take it that each soul can be a different thing, that there can be an infinite diversity of them within the general shape of consciousness.

I wrote an essay about the experience of eating peyote. The brittle, sun-dried sections of cactus flesh are called *buttons*. It began:

Cleaning the buttons is a wild experience. . . . You twist the knife point at the center of the dried disc of cactus. Suddenly blond silky fur begins to roil from the knife tip. Curls and twists of it fall to the table top. The fur comes out yellow-brown where it is old and dirty, and then the newly uncovered silver locks tumble out from the heart of the button. (In among the strands are tiny seeds where once there was a white-pink blossom like a daisy.) Next the gray tufts circling the center of the button are picked off. Then you eat the cactus flesh. A mystery of the organic is cast like a benign shadow on the experience to come.

The five peyote buttons that began that adventure of consciousness—which was like the ascent of a Himalayan mountain—were given to me by the mystic painter and photographer Wallace Berman. Berman had recently moved to San Francisco to escape harassment by the police in Los Angeles. A show of his art had been raided because of a photograph—in a templelike wooden sculpture—of the act of sexual penetration. The photograph could appear today with nothing remarkable about it—except its great beauty.

The day following my peyote high I was fortunate in having nearly perfect recall and wrote a long poem describing the vividness of the experience. Berman—my peyote father—published the first section of the poem as a broadside of his magazine *Semina*. Then it was published in my first book, *Hymns to St. Geryon*. This first section of the poem marks the beginning of the high:

PEYOTE POEM

Clear—the senses bright—sitting in the black chair—Rocker—
the white walls reflecting the color of clouds
moving over the sun. Intimacies! The rooms

not important—but like divisions of all space
of all hideousness and beauty. I hear
the music of myself and write it down

for no one to read. I pass fantasies as they
sing to me with Circe-Voices. I visit
among the peoples of myself and know all
I need to know.

I KNOW EVERYTHING! I PASS INTO THE ROOM

there is a golden bed radiating all light

the air is full of silver hangings and sheathes

I smile to myself. I know

all that there is to know. I see all there

is to feel. I am friendly with the ache
in my belly. The answer

to love is my voice. There is no Time!
No answers. The answer to feeling is my feeling.

The answer to joy is joy without feeling.

The room is a multicolored cherub
of air and bright colors. The pain in my stomach

is warm and tender. I am smiling. The pain
is many pointed, without anguish.

Light changes the room from yellows to violet!

The dark brown space behind the door is precious
intimate, silent and still. The birthplace
of Brahms. I know

all that I need to know. There is no hurry.

I read the meanings of scratched walls and cracked ceilings.

I am separate. I close my eyes in divinity and pain.

I blink in solemnity and unsolemn joy.

I smile at myself in my movements. Walking
I step higher in carefulness. I fill

space with myself. I see the secret and distinct
patterns of smoke from my mouth

I am without care part of all. Distinct.
I am separate from gloom and beauty. I see all.

(SPACIOUSNESS

And grim intensity—close within myself. No longer
a cloud
but flesh real as rock. Like Herakles

of primordial substance and vitality.
And not even afraid of the thing shorn of glamor

but accepting.
The beautiful things are not of ourselves

but I watch them. Among them.

And the Indian thing. It is true!
Here in my Apartment I think tribal thoughts.)

———————————————

STOMACHE!!!

There is no time. I am visited by a man
who is the god of foxes
there is dirt under the nails of his paw
fresh from his den.
We smile at one another in recognition.

I am free from Time. I accept it without triumph

—a fact.

Closing my eyes there are flashes of light.

My eyes won't focus but leap. I see that I have three feet.
I see seven places at once!
The floor slants—the room slopes
things melt
into each other. Flashes
of light

and meldings. I wait

seeing the physical thing pass.

I am on a mesa of time and space.

!STOM-ACHE!

Writing the music of life
in words.

Hearing the round sounds of the guitar
as colors.
Feeling the touch of flesh.

Seeing the loose chaos of words
on the page.
(ultimate grace)
(Sweet Yeats and his ball of hashish.)

My belly and I are two individuals
joined together
in life.

THIS IS THE POWERFUL KNOWLEDGE
we smile with it.

At the window I look into the blue-gray
gloom of dreariness.
I am warm. Into the dragon of space.
I stare into clouds seeing
their misty convolutions.

The whirls of vapor

I will small clouds out of existence.

They become fish devouring each other.

And change like Dante's holy spirits

becoming an osprey frozen skyhigh

to challenge me.

Of the hundred and fifty copies of *Peyote Poem* that Berman published, several were sold in City Lights Books in North Beach (the old bohemian and early Beat center near Chinatown in San Francisco). In the summer of 1958, Francis Crick, Nobel laureate and elucidator of the double helix of the DNA molecule, bought the broadside there. He included two lines of it in his book *Of Molecules and Men:*

THIS IS THE POWERFUL KNOWLEDGE
we smile with it

Crick's use of those lines shows the important, yet little known reaching out from science to poetry and from poetry to science that was part of the Beat movement. My friends of the late fifties were mostly poets and painters; however, my closest friend was a scientist—a visionary naturalist. He was an uncannily gifted observer, who introduced me to the nature of California. Having spent much of my childhood in the evergreen rain forests of Seattle, I expected Nature to be green trees and wide rivers. My naturalist friend showed me the subtleties of the California hills and savannas—and introduced me to falcons and pack rats and owls and coyotes. In childhood I had intended to be a naturalist or biologist and he helped me keep that stream of consciousness vital. My interest in biology has remained a constant thread through my searching.

Much of what the Beat Generation is about is nature—the landscape of nature in the case of Gary Snyder, the mind as nature in the case of Allen Ginsberg. Consciousness is a natural organic phenomenon. The Beats shared an interest in Nature, Mind, and Biology—areas that they expanded and held together with their radical political or antipolitical stance.

Three years before the peyote experience just described, I had given my first poetry reading with Allen Ginsberg, the Zen poet Philip Whalen, Gary Snyder, and the American Surrealist poet Philip Lamantia. The reading was in December 1955 at the Six Gallery in San Francisco. The Six Gallery was a cooperative art gallery run by young artists who centered around the San Francisco Art Institute. They were fiery artists who had either studied with Clyfford Still and Mark Rothko or with the newly emerging figurative painters. Their works ranged from huge drip and slash to minute precision smudges turning into faces. Earlier in the year poet Robert Duncan had given a staged reading of his play *Faust Foutu* (Faust Fucked) at the Six Gallery and, with the audacious purity of an Anarchist poet, he had stripped off his clothes at the end of the play.

On this night Kenneth Rexroth was master of ceremonies. This was the first time that Allen Ginsberg read *Howl*. Though I had known Allen for some months preceding, it was my first meeting with Gary Snyder and Philip Whalen. Lamantia did not read his poetry that night but instead recited works of the recently deceased John Hoffman—beautiful prose poems that left orange stripes and colored visions in the air.

The world that we tremblingly stepped out into in that decade was a bitter, gray one. But San Francisco was a special place. Rexroth said it was to the arts what Barcelona was to Spanish Anarchism. Still, there was no way, even in San Francisco, to escape the pressures of the war culture. We were locked in the Cold War and the first Asian debacle—the Korean War. My self-image in those years was of finding myself— young, high, a little crazed, needing a haircut, in an elevator with burly, crew-cutted, square-jawed eminences, staring at me like I was misplaced cannon fodder. We hated the war and the inhumanity and the coldness. The country had the feeling of martial law. An undeclared military state had leapt out of Daddy Warbucks' tanks and sprawled over the landscape. As artists we were oppressed and indeed the people of the nation were oppressed. There were certain of us (whether we were fearful or brave) who could not help speaking out—we had to speak. We knew we were poets and we had to speak out as poets. We saw that the art of poetry was essentially dead— killed by war, by academies, by neglect, by lack of love, and by disinterest. We knew we could bring it back to life. We could see what Pound had done—and Whitman, and Artaud, and D. H. Lawrence in his monumental poetry and prose.

The Six Gallery was a huge room that had been converted from an automobile repair shop into an art gallery. Someone had knocked together a little dais and was exhibiting sculptures by Fred Martin at the back of it—pieces of orange crates that had been swathed in muslin and dipped in plaster of paris to make splintered, sweeping shapes like pieces of surrealist furniture. A hundred and fifty enthusiastic people had come to hear us. Money was collected and jugs of wine were brought back for the audience. I hadn't seen Allen in a few weeks and I had not heard *Howl*—it was new to me. Allen began in a small and intensely lucid voice. At some point Jack Kerouac began shouting "GO" in cadence as Allen read it. In all of our memories no one had been so outspoken in poetry before—we had gone beyond a point of no return—and we were ready for it, for a point of no return. None of us wanted to go back to the gray, chill, militaristic silence, to the intellective void—to the land without poetry—to the spiritual drabness. We wanted to make it new and we wanted to invent it and the process of it as we went into it. We wanted voice and we wanted vision.

HOWL
for Carl Solomon

I

I saw the best minds of my generation destroyed by madness, starving hysteri-
    cal naked,
dragging themselves through the negro streets at dawn looking for an angry fix,

angelheaded hipsters burning for the ancient heavenly connection to the starry
    dynamo in the machinery of night,
who poverty and tatters and hollow-eyed and high sat up smoking in the su-
    pernatural darkness of cold-water flats floating across the tops of
    cities contemplating jazz,
who bared their brains to Heaven under the El and saw Mohammedan angels
    staggering on tenement roofs illuminated,
who passed through universities with radiant cool eyes hallucinating Arkansas
    and Blake-light tragedy among the scholars of war,
who were expelled from the academies for crazy & publishing obscene odes on
    the windows of the skull,
who cowered in unshaven rooms in underwear, burning their money in waste-
    baskets and listening to the Terror through the wall,
who got busted in their pubic beards returning through Laredo with a belt of
    marijuana for New York,
who ate fire in paint hotels or drank turpentine in Paradise Alley, death, or pur-
    gatoried their torsos night after night
with dreams, with drugs, with waking nightmares, alcohol and cock and end-
    less balls,
incomparable blind streets of shuddering cloud and lightning in the mind leap-
    ing toward poles of Canada & Paterson, illuminating all the mo-
    tionless world of Time between,
Peyote solidities of halls, backyard green tree cemetery dawns, wine drunken-
    ness over the rooftops, storefront boroughs of teahead joyride neon
    blinking traffic light, sun and moon and tree vibrations in the roar-
    ing winter dusks of Brooklyn, ashcan rantings and kind king light
    of mind,
who chained themselves to subways for the endless ride from Battery to holy
    Bronx on benzedrine until the noise of wheels and children brought
    them down shuddering mouth-wracked and battered bleak of
    brain all drained of brilliance in the drear light of Zoo,
who sank all night in submarine light of Bickford's floated out and sat through
    the stale beer afternoon in desolate Fugazzi's, listening to the crack
    of doom on the hydrogen jukebox,
who talked continuously seventy hours from park to pad to bar to Bellevue to
    museum to the Brooklyn Bridge,
a lost battalion of platonic conversationalists jumping down the stoops off fire
    escapes off windowsills off Empire State out of the moon,

yacketayakking screaming vomiting whispering facts and memories and anec-
    dotes and eyeball kicks and shocks of hospitals and jails and wars,
whole intellects disgorged in total recall for seven days and nights with brilliant
    eyes, meat for the Synagogue cast on the pavement,
who vanished into nowhere Zen New Jersey leaving a trail of ambiguous pic-
    ture postcards of Atlantic City Hall,
suffering Eastern sweats and Tangerian bone-grindings and migraines of China
    under junk-withdrawal in Newark's bleak furnished room,
who wandered around and around at midnight in the railroad yard wondering
    where to go, and went, leaving no broken hearts,
who lit cigarettes in boxcars boxcars boxcars racketing through snow toward
    lonesome farms in grandfather night,
who studied Plotinus Poe St. John of the Cross telepathy and bop kaballa be-
    cause the cosmos instinctively vibrated at their feet in Kansas. . . .

Ginsberg read on to the end of the poem, which left us
standing in wonder, or cheering and wondering, but knowing
at the deepest level that a barrier had been broken, that a hu-
man voice and body had been hurled against the harsh wall of
America and its supporting armies and navies and academies
and institutions and ownership systems and power-support
bases.

A week or so later I told Allen that *Howl* was like *Queen
Mab* — Shelley's first long poem. *Howl* was Allen's metamor-
phosis from quiet, brilliant, burning bohemian scholar trapped
by his flames and repressions to epic vocal bard. Shelley had
made the same transformation.

Also that night Gary Snyder, bearded and neat, a rugged
young man of nature at age twenty-five, read his scholarly and
ebullient nature poem, *A Berry Feast.*

A Berry Feast
For Joyce and Homer Matson

1
Fur the color of mud, the smooth loper
Crapulous old man, a drifter,
Praises! of Coyote the Nasty, the fat
Puppy that abused himself, the ugly gambler,
Bringer of goodies.

      In bearshit find it in August,
      Neat pile on the fragrant trail, in late
      August, perhaps by a Larch tree
      Bear has been eating the berries.
            high meadow, late summer, snow gone
      Blackbear
            eating berries, married
To a woman whose breasts bleed
From nursing the half-human cubs.

      Somewhere of course there are people
      collecting and junking, gibbering all day,

"Where I shoot my arrows
"There is the sunflower's shade
        —song of the rattlesnake
        coiled in the boulder's groin
"K'ak, k'ak, k'ak!
        sang Coyote. Mating with
        humankind—

The Chainsaw falls for boards of pine,
Suburban bedrooms, block on block
Will waver with this grain and knot,
The maddening shapes will start and fade
Each morning when commuters wake—
Joined boards hung on frames,
                a box to catch the biped in.

       and shadow swings around the tree
Shifting on the berrybush
      from leaf to leaf across each day
The shadow swings around the tree.

2

    Three, down, through windows
    Dawn leaping cats, all barred brown, grey
    Whiskers aflame
        bits of mouse on the tongue

    Washing the coffeepot in the river
        the baby yelling for breakfast,
    Her breasts, black-nippled, blue-veined, heavy,
    Hung through the loose shirt
        squeezed, with the free hand
          white jet in three cups.
    Cats at dawn
        derry derry down

Creeks wash clean where trout hide
We chew the black plug
Sleep on needles through long afternoons
       "you shall be owl
       "you shall be sparrow
       "you will grow thick and green, people
       "will eat you, you berries!
Coyote: shot from the car, two ears,
A tail, bring bounty.

    Clanks of tread
        oxen of Shang
        moving the measured road

Bronze bells at the throat
Bronze balls on the horns, the bright Oxen
Chanting through sunlight and dust
        wheeling logs down hills
       into heaps,
           the yellow

Fat-snout Caterpillar, tread toppling forward
Leaf on leaf, roots in gold volcanic dirt.

When
Snow melts back
        from the trees
Bare branches   knobbed pine twigs
       hot sun on wet flowers
Green shoots of huckleberry
Breaking through snow.

3

Belly stretched taut in a bulge
Breasts swelling as you guzzle beer, who wants
            Nirvana?
Here is water, wine, beer
Enough books for a week
A mess of afterbirth,
A smell of hot earth, a warm mist
Steams from the crotch

"You can't be killers all your life
"The people are coming—
      —and when Magpie
Revived him, limp rag of fur in the river
Drowned and drifting, fish-food in the shallows,
"Fuck you!" sang Coyote
       and ran.

Delicate blue-black, sweeter from meadows
Small and tart in the valleys, with light blue dust
Huckleberries scatter through pine woods
Crowd along gullies, climb dusty cliffs,
Spread through the air by birds;
Find them in droppings of bear.

"Stopped in the night
"Ate hot pancakes in a bright room
"Drank coffee, read the paper
"In a strange town, drove on,

singing, as the drunkard swerved the car
"Wake from your dreams, bright ladies!
"Tighten your legs, squeeze demons from
        the crotch with rigid thighs
"Young red-eyed men will come
"With limp erections, snuffling cries
"To dry your stiffening bodies in the sun!

Woke at the beach. Grey dawn,
Drenched with rain. One naked man
Frying his horsemeat on a stone.

4
Coyote yaps, a knife!
Sunrise on yellow rocks.
People gone, death no disaster,
Clear sun in the scrubbed sky
            empty and bright
Lizards scurry from darkness
We lizards sun on yellow rocks.

See, from the foothills
Shred of river glinting, trailing,
To flatlands, the city:
            glare of haze in the valley horizon
Sun caught on glass gleams and goes.
From cool springs under cedar
On his haunches, white grin,
            long tongue panting, he watches:

Dead city in dry summer,
Where berries grow.

Snyder's gloss on the poem reads: "The berry feast is a first-fruits celebration that consumes a week of mid-August on the Warm Springs Indian Reservation in Oregon. Coyote is the name of the Trickster-Hero of the mythology of that region."

What I hear in the poem is Snyder's concern that we must, as Charles Olson proposed in "Call Me Ishmael," change time itself into space through an alchemic act. Then we may move in it and step outside of the disaster that we have wreaked upon the environment and upon our phylogenetic selves. Snyder looks back to the Indians with their hunting and gathering Paleolithic culture—and recounts the joy of their berry feast in a song that is like those of ancient Greece. It is dancelike and reminds me of how the Chorus dithyrambed in the wine feast to another Trickster-God, Dionysus. Snyder also looks to the measured, eudaemonic semistasis—the slow-moving post-Neolithic history of the Shang Dynasty in China with its tinkle of ox bells. To these he compares the machine harvesting of our forests—trees being mowed down to make boxes for bipeds, with no feelings for Nature. Throughout the poem there is the solidity of a physical romance with a woman and the joy in the warmth of the flesh of her arms around him—and the sight and sense and taste of the berries.

Even in those days Philip Whalen was a big man. As I watched him read, the meaning of his metamorphic poem gradually began to sink in. We laughed as the poem's intent clarified. Here was a poem by a poet-scholar (who is now a Zen priest as well as a major American poet) with a multiple thrust. Whalen was using the American speech that William Carlos Williams instructed us to use, but he put it to a different use. Whalen's poems were not only naturalistic portrayals of objects and persons transformed by poetry—they also used American speech for the naked joy of portraying metamorphosis and of exemplifying and aiding change in the universe. They manifested a positive Whiteheadian joy in shifting and in processes. Whalen read this poem with a mock seriousness that was at once biting, casual, and good natured.

"Plus Ça Change . . ."

What are you doing?

  I am coldly calculating

I didn't ask for a characterization.
Tell me what we're going to do.

  That's what I'm coldly calculating.

You had better say "plotting" or "scheming"
You never could calculate without a machine.

  Then I'm brooding. Presently
  A plot will hatch.

Who are you trying to kid?

  Be nice.

  (SILENCE)

Listen. Whatever we do from here on out
Let's for God's sake not look at each other
Keep our eyes shut and the lights turned off—
We won't mind touching if we don't have to see.

  I'll ignore those preposterous feathers.

Say what you please, we brought it all on ourselves
But nobody's going out of his way to look.

  Who'd recognize us now?

We'll just pretend we're used to it.
(Watch out with that goddamned tail!)

Pull the shades down. Turn off the lights.
Shut your eyes.

(SILENCE)

There is no satisfactory explanation.
You can talk until you're blue

Just how much bluer can I get?

Well, save breath you need to cool

Will you please shove the cuttlebone a little closer?

All right, until the perfumes of Arabia

Grow cold. Ah! Sunflower seeds!

Will you listen, please? I'm trying to make
A rational suggestion. Do you mind?

Certainly not. Just what *shall* we tell the children?

"*Plus Ça Change . . .*" hangs in space making a shape like a
sculpture. Each reading of it is a little different. You can see
them changing into parakeets. The poem is created like a Goya
engraving or a Sung Dynasty landscape painting with the
proper number of strokes, not too many and not too few. It is
concise, powerful, and humorous. It exhibits faith in change to
the extent of desiring change. Exuberant. Olson said in para-
phrase of Herakleitos:

What does not change / is the will to change.

The Six Gallery reading was open to the world and the
world was welcome. There were poets and Anarchists and

Stalinists and professors and painters and bohemians and visionaries and idealists and grinning cynics.

I had been fascinated by the thought and the poetry of the French maudite, antiphysical, mystic poet Antonin Artaud, who had died toothless and, it is said, mad in Paris in 1948, only seven years before our Six Gallery reading. One of my first exchanges with Philip Lamantia on meeting him in 1954 was to ask where I could find more works by Artaud. I was fascinated by Artaud's visionary gnosticism. I was looking for a way beyond the objectism of American poetry and the post-Symbolism of French poetry and I sensed that Artaud's poetry, a breakthrough incarnate, was a way into the open field of poetry and into the open shape of verse and into the physicality of thought. I was looking for a verbal and physical athletics where poetry could be achieved. In their direct statement to my nerves, lines of Artaud's were creating physical tensions, and gave me ideas for entries into a new mode of verse.

One phrase of Artaud's fascinated me: "It is not possible that in the end the miracle will not occur." I replied with a poem I read at the Six Gallery.

POINT LOBOS: ANIMISM

It is possible my friend,
If I have had a fat belly
That the wolf lives on fat
Gnawing slowly
Through a visceral night of rancor.
It is possible that the absence of pain
May be so great
That the possibility of care
May be impossible.

Perhaps to know pain.
Anxiety, rather than the fear
Of the fear of anxiety.
This talk of miracles!

Of Animism:
I have been in a spot so full of spirits
That even the most joyful animist
Brooded
When all in sight was less to be cared about
Than death
And there was no noise in the ears
That mattered.
(I knelt in the shade
By a cold salt pool
And felt the entrance of hate
On many legs,
The soul like a clambering
Water vascular system.

No scuttling could matter
Yet I formed in my mind
The most beautiful
Of maxims.
How could I care
For your illness or mine?)
This talk of bodies!

It is impossible to speak
Of lupine or tulips
When one may read
His name
Spelled by the mold on the stumps
When the forest moves about one.

Heel. Nostril.
Light. Light! Light!
This is the bird's song
You may tell it
To your children.

I did not fear obscurity in my poetry because I had come to
believe that the way to the universal was by means of the most
intensely personal. I believed that what we truly share with
others lies in the deepest, most personal, even physiological
core—and not in the outer social world of speech that is used
for grooming and transactions. Further, as Clyfford Still, a
contemporary of Jackson Pollock and a heroic Abstract Ex-
pressionist, said, "Demands for communication are presump-
tuous and irrelevant." Jazz and bop had convinced me that
poets might also communicate by music, by sound, like The-
lonius Monk, Charlie Parker, Miles Davis.

Point Lobos: Animism has a tight, small sound—not entire-
ly different from the sound of a Romantic sonnet. Its intent is
personal and specific. I hoped to alter the lyric form into a new
shape and to allow a subject to create the exterior shape as well
as the sound and music. I wanted to tell of my feelings of hun-
ger, of emptiness, and of epiphany. I hoped to state the sharp-
ness of a demonic joy that I found in a place of incredible beau-
ty on the coast of Northern California. I wanted to say how I
was overwhelmed by the sense of animism—and how every-
thing (breath, spot, rock, ripple in the tidepool, cloud, and
stone) was alive and spirited. It was a frightening and joyous
awareness of my undersoul. I say *undersoul* because I did not
want to join Nature by my mind but by my viscera—my belly.
The German language has two words, *Geist* for the soul of
man and *Odem* for the spirit of beasts. Odem is the under-
soul. I was becoming sharply aware of it.

I was also interested in the subtle, Chagall-like aspects of Nature that are part of the life of the city. Even in an apartment one can think tribal thoughts, or human, mammal thoughts—or soft, beautiful, Nature thoughts that tell of the oneness, the monism, of nature. Ernst Haeckel and Alfred North Whitehead believed that the universe is a single organism—that the whole thing is alive and that its existence is its sacredness and its breathing. If all is divine and alive—and if everything is the Uncarved Block of the Taoists—then all of it and any part is beauteous (or possibly hideous) and of enormous value. It is beyond proportion. One cannot say that a virus is less special or less divine than a wolf or butterfly or rose blossom. One cannot say that a star or cluster of galaxies is more important—has more proportion—than a chipmunk or floorboard. This recognition is always within us.

City nature could be as beautiful as Klee's work, or Chagall's—and it could be without the limits of proportion. I read this poem at the Six Gallery.

Night Words: The Ravishing

How beautiful things are in a beautiful room
At night
Without proportion
A black longhaired cat with a sensitive human face
A white robe hangs on the wall
Like a soft ghost
Without proportion
Songs flit through my head
The room is calm and still and cool
Blue gray stillness
Without proportion
The plants are alive
Giving off votive oxygen

To the benevolent pictures above them
Songs flit through my head
I am taken with insomnia
With ambrosial insomnia
And songs flit through my head
The room is softened
Things are without proportion
And I must sleep

Another piece I read at the Six Gallery was simply titled *Poem*. There was no further title because it was as far as I had been able to go in poetry. It said much of what I wanted to say in a myriad thrust.

In high school I had written cadenced, imagistic, and even pictographic free verse through the inspiration of Pound, Yeats, cummings, Kenneth Patchen, and William Carlos Williams. Later, I went through experiments in formal genre: sonnets, ballads, villanelles. Now I wished to express the intensity and vividness of my own perceptions and the *manner* in which impressions linked themselves in the exciting swirl that I called my consciousness. I believed that consciousness was physical and physiological and athletic—and that it rode, and moved, and strode, and had the capacity for laughter and for song. I knew that consciousness was part of the physiological body and not separate from the rest of nature—that it was wound through, woven in, bursting out from, and pouring through all nature.

Communication was not as important to me as expression. To speak and move was the most important thing.

POEM

Linked part to part, toe to knee, eye to thumb
Motile, feral, a blockhouse of sweat
The smell of the hunt's
A stench, . . . my foetor.
The eye a bridegroom of torture
Colors are linked by spirit
Euglena, giraffe, frog
Creatures of grace—Rishi
Of their own right.

As I walk my legs say to me 'Run
There is joy in swiftness'
As I speak my tongue says to me 'Sing
There is joy in thought,
The size of the word
Is its own flight from crabbedness.'

And the leaf is an ache
And love an ache in the back.
The stone a creature.

A PALISADE

The inside whitewashed.

. . . . . .
. . . . . .
. . . . . .
. . . . . !

A pale tuft of grass.

My concerns in this brief lyric are as various as Buddha's Fire Sermon (that the eye is a bridegroom of torture), physical anthropology (that we are linked part to part), and sexuality (that love is an ache in the back). The poem was also concerned with its own structure. I thought of it as a real PHYS-ICAL OBJECT. I was not just making a lyric about feelings, or about emotions, or objects. I tried to create the poem in the shape of a palisade, a stockade. Influenced by Oriental thought (especially in Oriental painting) I used *ma*, the negative space in landscape, as a silence in the poem. There are four lines of dots utilizing silent time as space in the poem. The four lines of dots are followed by an exclamation point. The last line, "A pale tuft of grass," is an image from the stockade but, secretly, a whisper from Whitman.

At the Six Gallery I also read a poem that sprang from an article in *Time* magazine (April 1954). Excerpts from the article used to preface the poem say:

Killer whales. . . . Savage sea cannibals up to thirty feet long with teeth like bayonets . . . one was caught with fourteen seals and thir-teen porpoises in its belly . . . often tear at boats and nets . . . de-stroyed thousands of dollars worth of fishing tackle. . . . Icelandic government appealed to the U.S., which has thousands of men sta-tioned at a lonely NATO airbase on the subarctic island. Seventy-nine bored G.I.'s responded with enthusiasm. Armed with rifles and machine guns one posse of Americans climbed into four small boats and in one morning wiped out a pack of 100 killers. . . .

First the killers were rounded up into tight formation with con-centrated machine gun fire, then moved out again one by one, for the final blast which would kill them . . . as one was wounded, the others would set upon it and tear it to pieces with their jagged teeth.

I was horrified and angry when I read about the slaughter and I wrote:

FOR THE DEATH OF 100 WHALES

Hung midsea
Like a boat mid-air
The Liners boiled their pastures:
The Liners of flesh,
The Arctic steamers.

Brains the size of a football
Mouths the size of a door.

The sleek wolves
Mowers and reapers of sea kine.
THE GIANT TADPOLES
(Meat their algae)
Lept
Like sheep or children.
Shot from the sea's bore.

Turned and twisted
(Goya!!)
Flung blood and sperm.
Incense.
Gnashed at their tails and brothers,
Cursed Christ of mammals,
Snapped at the sun,
Ran for the sea's floor.

Goya! Goya!
Oh Lawrence
No angels dance those bridges.
OH GUN! OH BOW!
There are no churches in the waves,
No holiness,
No passages or crossings
From the beasts' wet shore.

The slaughter of the whales was a murder that I thought only Goya could have portrayed in his *Horrors of War*. I called on D. H. Lawrence at the end to be the tutelary figure of the poem because of his description of the copulation of whales and his imaginings of the angels moving from body to body in the mammoth act.

And over the bridge of the whale's strong phallus, linking the won-
    der of whales
the burning archangels under the sea keep passing, back and forth,
    keep passing archangels of bliss
from him to her, from her to him, great Cherubim
that wait on whales in mid-ocean, suspended in the waves of the sea
great heaven of whales in the waters, old hierarchies.
                                        from *Whales Weep Not*

Years later, at the United Nations Environmental Confer-ence in Stockholm in 1972, Gary Snyder and I were among the contingent of independent lobbyists (led by Project Jonah and Stewart Brand) who took it upon themselves to represent whales, Indians, and the freedom of the diversity of the envi-ronment. We participated in whale demonstrations in Stock-holm and immediately following the conference I returned to San Francisco and staged a pro-whale demonstration. At the Stockholm conference Snyder wrote and distributed a poem, *Mother Earth: Her Whales*, which reads in part:

North America, Turtle Island, taken by invaders
        who wage war around the world.
May ants, may abalone, otters, wolves and elk
Rise! and pull away their giving
        from the robot nations.

Solidarity. The People.
Standing Tree People!

Flying Bird People!
Swimming Sea People!
Four legged, two-legged, people!

How can the head-heavy power-hungry politic scientist
Government   two world   Capitalist-Imperialist
Third-World   Communist   paper-shuffling male
       non-farmer   jet-set   bureaucrats
Speak for the green of the leaf? Speak for the soil?

(Ah Margaret Mead . . . do you sometimes dream of Samoa?)

The robots argue how to parcel out our Mother Earth
To last a little longer
                    like vultures flapping
belching, gurgling,
                    near a dying Doe.

In the late seventies, Robert Creeley, in *Desultory Days,*
which he called a "muskrat ramble," brought together many
threads, and presented a maturation of the Beat/Black Moun-
tain impulse. The poem resembles the Chinese *fu*—or rhyme
prose. It joins awareness of living environment, oneness of
time, deepening of consciousness, and myriad-mindedness. The
poem is dedicated to the naturalist Peter Warshall.

Desultory Days

Desultory days,
time's wandering
impermanences—

like, *what's for lunch,*
Mabel? Hunks
of unwilling

meat got chopped
from recalcitrant
beasts? "No tears

for this vision" —
nor huge strawberries
zapped from forlorn Texas,

too soon, too soon . . .
We will meet again
one day, we will

gather at the river
(Paterson perchance)
so turgidly oozes by,

etc. Nothing new in the world
but us, the human
parasite eats up

that self-defined reality
we talked about in
ages past. Now prophecy declares,

got to get on with it,
back to the farm, else die
in streets inhuman

'spite we made them every one.
Ah friends, before I die,
I want to sit awhile

upon this old world's knee,
yon charming hill, you see,
and dig the ambient breezes,

make of life
such gentle passing pleasure!
Were it then wrong

to avoid, as might be said,
the heaped-up canyons of the dead—
L.A.'s drear smut, and N.Y.C.'s

crunched millions? I don't know.
It seems to me
what can salvation be

for less than 1%
of so-called population
is somehow latent fascism

of the soul. What leaves behind
those other people,
like they say,

reneges on Walter Whitman's
19th century Mr. Goodheart's
Lazy Days and Ways In Which

we might still *save the world.*
I loved it but
I never could believe it—

rather, the existential
terror of New England
countrywoman, Ms.

Dickinson: "The Brain, within its Groove
Runs evenly—and true—
But let a Splinter swerve—

"'Twere easier for You—//
To put a Current back—
When Floods have slit the Hills—

"And scooped a Turnpike for Themselves—
And Trodden out the Mills—"
moves me. My mind

to me a nightmare is—
that thought of days,
years, went its apparent way

without itself, with
no other company than thought.
So—*born to die*—why

take everything with us?
Why the meagerness
of life deliberately,

why the patience
when of no use,
and the anger, when it is?

I am no longer
one man—
but an old one

who is human again
after a long time,
feels the meat contract,

or stretch, upon bones,
hates to be alone
but can't stand interruption.

Funny
how it all works out,
and Asia is

after all *how much money*
it costs —
either to buy or to sell it.

Didn't they have a
world too? But then
they don't look like us,

do they? But they'll get us,
someone will — they'll find us,
they won't leave us here

just to die
by ourselves
all alone?

II.
THE SHAPE OF ENERGY

1.

Hammering It Out

Every animal is an end in itself — it comes forth perfect from
Nature's womb and begets young that are perfect. All limbs
develop according to eternal laws, and even the rarest of forms
mysteriously preserves the archetype. Thus every mouth is skilled
to grasp the kind of food that suits the body; whether the jaw be
feeble and toothless, or strongly toothed, in every case a suitable
organ conveys the food to the rest of the limbs. Every foot, too,
whether long or short, moves in complete harmony with the
animal's intentions and needs. Thus for each of her children the
Mother ordains pure and entire health; for no living limbs ever
function in contradiction to each other, and all act in the interests
of life. In this way the animal's shape is determined by its way of
life, and the way of life, in its turn, exerts in all cases a powerful
influence upon the shape. Thus ordered development displays
both constancy and a tendency to change because of external
forces. The internal energy, however, of the nobler sort of
creatures finds itself bounded by the sacred circle of living
development. These are bounds which no god can extend, and
Nature honours them: for only within such limitations has
perfection ever been possible.

Goethe, *The Metamorphosis of Animals,*
prose translation by David Luke, *The Penguin Poets.*

This section is entitled "Hammering It Out"—but it no more hammers everything out than the first essay made enough scratches through the paint to show the surface beneath.

This section raises questions regarding the biological basis of poetry and seeks insights into poetic history derived from work in the field; for the field of poetry, as Robert Duncan saw, opened swiftly and like a blossom. Though there was much history for it, we had been present in a spurt and a SURGE. There was a surprising broadening of the field into substrates that were not earlier imagined to be there for the viable creation of poetry, and, strangely enough, into areas that did not seem to exist before poems were written about them. The poems defined new areas.

The last volume of Olson's *Maximus Poems*—like Mallarmé's unfinished, open-ended *Le Livre*—is, in part, a poem about the architecture of the poem itself. In that way it is much like an organism. A creature is about itself. A living organism is perceived as a complex chunk, or lump, or bulk, or motile body of reproductive plasm. And of course it is that. The most rewarding view of the organism, and of organically complex works of art, is that which is comprised of several equally valid views.

A way of seeing an organism, other than as a lump or bulk of self-perpetuating protoplasm (and there's nothing wrong

43

with that), is the view that the organism is, in itself, a tissue or veil between itself and the environment. And, it is not only the tissue between itself and the environment—it is also simultaneously the environment itself. The organism is what Whitehead and Olson would think of as a point of novelty comprehending itself or experiencing itself both proprioceptively and at its tissue's edges and at any of its conceivable surfaces.

There is, in fact, a central force in the organism and it IS the environment.

The organism is a swirl of environment in what the Taoists call the Uncarved Block of time and space (a universe in which time and space are not separated into intersecting facets by measured incidents).

The veil, the tissue (or the lump or bulk), is created by the storms from which it protects itself—and is itself the ongoing storm. Herakleitos saw it as a storm of fire, the raging of an active and energetic principle.

The organism is a constellation (like a constellation of stars or molecules) of resonances between itself and the outer environment. The organism is a physical pattern of reflections and counterreflections that we call a body and we see it clearly as a physiology. Ourselves. A rose bush. An amoeba. An apple.

It is our overabstracted nature that does not see the complexity, or feel the complexity, of the body. Charles Olson realized that when he wrote his essay, "Projective Verse." Projective verse—like action painting—comes from a complex body. Olson saw a breath and energy interaction creating the poetic line. The breath, like the word, is part of the body. One must hold a deep view of our organism in order to search for the real, the meatly, the physiological STANCE. Metaphorically, there is a solid ledge of our own substrate from which we must leap out like a predator (or dart from gracefully like a gatherer) in order to create true poetry. As a model we see hunting creatures (such as leopards, salmon, wolves) looking out, phylogenetically unhampered, into the Uncarved Block. After the look they take their leap.

Before more of this, one digression: In his introduction to Darwin's *Origin of Species* Richard E. Leakey writes, "Some paleontologists, notably Stephen Jay Gould of Harvard, think the fossil evidence suggests that at various stages in the history of life evolution has progressed rapidly—in 'spurts'—and that major branching in the evolutionary tree has occurred at these points. This may have occurred because an evolving group had reached a stage in its organization at which it had an advantage over other groups and, once this threshold had been passed, it was able to radiate rapidly to exploit a variety of niches. Or a 'spurt' may have followed from a widespread change of climate, or from the extinction of another group of species leaving many niches vacant."

Leakey and Gould appended this extension to Darwin's thought because in his formulation of the concept of evolution Darwin was inclined to see a relatively steady state of advance. Today, with almost no alteration of Darwin's insight, we may also see the wave motion of feedback and reflection and counterreflection in the progress towards complexity and diversity.

A theory of the development of poetry surely will reflect poetry's origins in the body and in the growing complexity and diversity of the body. Thus the "feeled" grows—the *field* on which poetry grows is the *feeled* . . . the felt. The *veldt*.

If that sounds circular, like a definition defining itself, that is because it reflects the nature both of poetry and of the organism that creates it.

There is no separation between body and mind.

A poem that moved me, both as a mammal recognizing myself and as a reader recognizing fleshly thought in poetry, was published in the Spring 1954 *Black Mountain Review*. Paul Blackburn is the author.

The Search

I have been looking for this animal for three days now
                    and four nights
                    not finding him.
Probing into the corners of my mind to find him,
glancing into store windows and into the faces of women.

            Sometimes I think it is a bird
                    but then again not.
            Once I was sure it was a lizard
facing my left trouser-leg at a pet-shop window,
                    crouched
with his tongue darting out in primeval coldness.
But I found myself looking again the following day.

So neither very-hot blooded nor cold blooded,
                    those early creations.
It is small, it has four legs and fur.

I saw it, almost, under the dark brows
of a Puerto Rican child in the street.
                    A garment worker.
            Her belly was small and round
                    and it was growing.
But she saw I looked and the thing changed in her eyes
                    and it was a woman.
I have a woman. That's not what I look for now.

                    My cat gave me a clue.
He was lying on his back, his feet in the air
                    asleep. The thing was
            the mixture of attitude in his face,
the sublime trust and disdain, careless, sure.

            Turned out it was a hamster.
You find them in cages with treadmills, which
                    seems to me a symbol.

This from a magazine someplace
              with a set of pictures.
Mine was not in a treadmill. He
lay on a ledge in the sun in the window
              of a shoe repair shop on Sixth Avenue,
his legs stretched out behind him, sideways,
for he lay on one side in the sun
washing his face with one paw like a cat
                            ignoring the traffic.

              And having found him out
I didn't know what to make of him, except that
he was a small fat rodent and looked careless,
that he was a mammal and sure.

What an enormous change there was between that almost casual post-troubadour poem and another poem I was reading at the time, Hart Crane's *A Name for All. The Search* rippled with sinuous verbal muscularity. Crane's poem gleamed brightly with the physicality of a more formal high art:

A Name for All

Moonmoth and grasshopper that flee our page
And still wing on, untarnished of the name
We pinion to your bodies to assuage
Our envy of your freedom—we must maim

Because we are usurpers, and chagrined—
And take the wing and scar it in the hand.
Names we have, even, to clap on the wind;
But we must die, as you, to understand.

I dreamed that all men dropped their names, and sang
As only they can praise, who build their days
With fin and hoof, with wing and sweetened fang
Struck free and holy in one Name always.

But it was not the difference between two such artful works, widely spread in the evolutionary radiation of poetry, that intrigued me, as much as another possibility.

I answered Blackburn in 1955:

SHORT SONG

The searching. Day after day a search.
No lumberjack or songbird I,
travelling through my bronchi
and leaping
out on the world
FLINT
through mouth, through hands.

The air flows gathering all to intensity.

A LONG STRIDE THROUGH THE SPRUCE.

(The breakup, the shattering,
flies through mountain, through water.
The forms left cleaner: compost heap or reed.
. . . .
. . . .
All that is left on the ears—a chuckle.)

This confused and aspiring poem was one that I could not include in my first book. Like Blackburn, I was searching for the animal—my mammal—looking for it in theories of breath and line and Edward Sapir and jazz and sources such as Whitman and the Fire Sermon of Gautama Buddha.

What I could see so clearly, however, in that poem of Blackburn's, and to some degree in the poetry of Black Mountaineers and pre-Beat Beats and experimenters, was that there were new paths open—new trails through the spruce on which to make long strides.

There was in Blackburn's *The Search* both a step down from Whitman—and a stride to what was broader—a changing of Walt Whitman's grasping for scale into a warm mammal personalism. I was excited because it was about a search. I also wanted a change of Whitman's scale, without loss of it, and I wanted it to be to my own organism.

I believed that the cosmic scale of Whitman's *Song of Myself,* the experience seed of *Leaves of Grass,* was already manifest and was demonstrated within visionary precepts. The awareness that we are all without proportion, and that all living beings are proportionless, seemed natural. We who felt deeply in the cold fifties were monists and animists. The fifties were most distinguished in the mental field by the creative energy of the artists and poets, and by war neurosis by the country at large.

Looking at Blackburn's poem *The Search,* one could believe that Walt Whitman's Shivaic temple of the Cosmos was here—that one would lose no vertical aspiration by accepting it. There was also possible now a lateral step into the mammal-personal—and maybe into the subjective-personal rather than the weeping wall or chest-beating mode.

If that was true, then what would be more important than to look down? What would be more personal? I was standing on my feet. My feet stood on all of the bodies that came before me. My body was the development of all those countless human, prehuman, great-great-grandfather bodies before me, stretching back to the first assemblage and constellation of replicating atoms in a bizarre molecule. I *was* my body—ME. Scratching at the Beat Surface, I found it out line by line, and perception by perception, and with the grief of multitudinous blind alleys and new starts.

Olson and I were both looking for the world from which poetry comes. That world is a substrate within us—and not a simple dimensional one—not a flat plane.

We ourselves, at our fundament, are composed of complex proteins whose enfolding and use of space resembles a crumpled helix and its double. We are looking for a point that is both inside of ourselves because we are an organism and outside of ourselves because, as organisms, we are created of the environment in an exquisite complex of motions. Another society might say that we were looking for the *spirit area* from which poetry comes—or from which it arrives—or from which verse is energized.

I expressed this in a poem:

FOR CHARLES

1.

THE

LUMPS

THAT
WE

ARE!

((MOVING

through
these

ROMANTIC
STORMS

OF DARK BLUE
and silver waves)))

The lumps that we are
are reflections

and counter-reflections
of the winds and breakers

themselves . . .

2.

THERE

IS

A

CENTRAL
FORCE

in
us

&

it's
everywhere.

WE
ARE
ALWAYS

STRIDING into it!

It blows in our ears
and eyes,

WE
ARE

the core of it.

After working with traditional English sources in Yeats, Pound, Blake, and Shelley, I studied poetry with Robert Duncan in the midfifties. There I found myself in a thicket of experiments with the consciousness, the physicality, and the mentality of poetry—and also in a literary milieu. I met Jonathan Williams, who introduced me to works of Creeley and of Olson (as well as personally to Kenneth Patchen). Duncan insisted on truth without the mask of formal art—on the poem being true to itself first of all. In *Letters,* his ground-breaking book, the effort to produce a line that was consciousness itself, with variable long and short lines, worked on my imagination. With fascination, and no great ease, I came to Olson's poetry. By then my introspective work in the biological fundament of poetry had led to essays like "Revolt" and "Phi Upsilon Kappa."

Many poets in that period were creating, projectively, their own systems—their own momentary system of poetics. We were aware that a system should be momentary—that it was not immortal, not permanent. The system was a tool—like the electron microscope—that could lead to the insight and the discovery of new poetry.

As I came to understand Olson personally and through his work I began to object to his concept of "anagogic," of poetry *leading out.* I believed that the spring of poetry must be more physical, more genetic, more based in flesh, and have less relationship to culture. It must, I discovered for myself, be something that occurs before the anagogic, something that happens before the *leading out*—it must be "pre-anagogic." A terrible name, but perhaps in its clumsiness a useful tool, one that was so knobby that it might have previously unsuspected handholds on it. The idea was certainly not subtle, but it felt big to me.

To create poetry one must have a system—or an antisystem, or a *systemless system.* A *systemless system* is one that alters itself in the waves with a living anarchism—like the evolution through scores of millions of years of the Portuguese man-of-war and other colonial coelenterates, or the migration systems worked out by the bison or the wildebeest. Each individual's actions and patterns are a recapitulation of the old deep patterns in the meat.

In the search for a systemless system I took a negative view of systems *per se.* In the early sixties I wrote a mad sonnet:

THE PANSY

SYSTEMS ARE DEATH!   THE BLACK AND YELLOW PANSY
HAS NO RULES
but stares with catlike face from clumpy leaves
—a shaggy shapely head upon a tiny stalk.
Look, the black is purple.
The jowls droop but the forehead raises high.
A single central eye where petals meet!
The face is flamey splash!
IS THERE ANY LAW BUT LIFE?

_____

Need there be a code but that of sigh or cry
or dream, or silence, or of movement or of growth?
SWEET AND BITTER JOIN
to lift
a higher thing
that moves in air.
What does *system* mean
to molecules of dry and moist?

_ _ _ _ _ _ _ _ _ _ _ _ _ _ _ _ _ _ _ _

My mind is lovely as a spruce and I
and those who love me,
make it mine.

The secret about systems—is that all systems work. Almost any system, with intellective investment in it, is advantaged over no system. Another quality of systems is that they create bondage. They limit, they blur, they mystify. Meister Eckhart

reflected that the belief in God limits the ability to know God. If one has a system in which God can be known it makes an image of God that hides what God may be truly. One's system works; therefore one believes one has more than one has. The idea that one perceives what is truly there shows much faith in a system. Systems work in the short run and yet the long-lasting constellations are probably systemless systems. For instance, the turbulence of the universe, the evolution of life, and the perception-generation of art are long-lasting systemless systems.

The Yale biophysicist Harold Morowitz has as his general thesis in *Energy Flow in Biology* the proposition that "THE FLOW OF ENERGY THROUGH A SYSTEM ACTS TO ORGANIZE THAT SYSTEM" (my caps). This awareness links matter and energy into one insight, one vision.

The creation of projective verse is ideally the flowing or pouring of energy through the system (or *systemless system*) of Olson's concepts.

The systemless system must be loosely, yet complexly, looped, and allow for invention and stochastic structuring (and possibly chance) so that it may accommodate both Negative Capability and agnosia—knowing through not knowing. Such a system is a kind of deep spirit-thought and is capable of creating stepping stones through the torrent, and through the torment, of the search for vocal rage—for inspired and heightened expression.

It is the surge of our physical energy that carries us through—and we need no vanity about having it—it is an inheritance. It is also the surge that organizes the system into tribes. It spurts and it radiates. It is the energy that defines poetry. *The Kingfishers* is an ode to energy and of energy. Like us, the exterior is an extension of the interior. It is myriad, it is one.

The Kingfishers

1
What does not change / is the will to change

He woke, fully clothed, in his bed. He
remembered only one thing, the birds, how
when he came in, he had gone around the rooms
and got them back in their cage, the green one first,
she with the bad leg, and then the blue,
the one they had hoped was a male

Otherwise? Yes, Fernand, who had talked lispingly of Albers & Angkor Vat.
He had left the party without a word. How he got up, got into his coat,
I do not know. When I saw him, he was at the door, but it did not matter,
he was already sliding along the wall of the night, losing himself
in some crack of the ruins. That it should have been he who said, "The
                    kingfishers!
who cares
for their feathers
now?"

His last words had been, "The pool is slime." Suddenly everyone,
ceasing their talk, sat in a row around him, watched
they did not so much hear, or pay attention, they
wondered, looked at each other, smirked, but listened,
he repeated and repeated, could not go beyond his thought
"The pool   the kingfishers' feathers were wealth   why
did the export stop?"

It was then he left

2
I thought of the E on the stone, and of what Mao said
la lumiere"
              but the kingfisher

de l'aurore"
              but the kingfisher flew west
est devant nous!
              he got the color of his breast
              from the heat of the setting sun!

The features are, the feebleness of the feet (syndactylism of the 3rd & 4th digit)
the bill, serrated, sometimes a pronounced beak, the wings
where the color is, short and round, the tail
inconspicuous.

But not these things are the factors. Not the birds.
The legends are
legends. Dead, hung up indoors, the kingfisher
will not indicate a favoring wind,
or avert the thunderbolt. Nor, by its nesting,
still the waters, with the new year, for seven days.
It is true, it does nest with the opening year, but not on the waters.
It nests at the end of a tunnel bored by itself in a bank. There,
six or eight white and translucent eggs are laid, on fishbones
not on bare clay, on bones thrown up in pellets by the birds.

                         On these rejectamenta
(as they accumulate they form a cup-shaped structure) the young are born.
And, as they are fed and grow, this nest of excrement and decayed fish becomes
                         a dripping, fetid mass

Mao concluded:
              nous devons
                     nous lever
                            et agir!

3
When the attentions change / the jungle
leaps in
              even the stones are split
                     they rive

Or,
enter
that other conqueror we more naturally recognize
he so resembles ourselves

But the E
cut so rudely on that oldest stone
sounded otherwise,
was differently heard

as, in another time, were treasures used:

(and, later, much later, a fine ear thought
a scarlet coat)

       "of green feathers   feet, beaks and eyes
       of gold

       "animals likewise,
       resembling snails

       "a large wheel, gold, with figures of unknown four-foots,
       and worked with tufts of leaves, weight
       3800 ounces

       "last, two birds, of thread and featherwork, the quills
       gold, the feet
       gold, the two birds perched on two reeds
       gold, the reeds arising from two embroidered mounds,
       one yellow, the other
       white.

           "And from each reed hung
           seven feathered tassels.

In this instance, the priests
(in dark cotton robes, and dirty,
their dishevelled hair matted with blood, and flowing wildly

over their shoulders)
rush in among the people, calling on them
to protect their gods

And all now is war
where so lately there was peace,
and the sweet brotherhood, the use
of tilled fields.

4
Not one death but many,
not accumulation but change, the feed-back proves, the feed-back is
the law

>Into the same river no man steps twice
>When fire dies air dies
>No one remains, nor is, one

Around an appearance, one common model, we grow up
many. Else how is it,
if we remain the same,
we take pleasure now
in what we did not take pleasure before? love
contrary objects? admire and/or find fault? use
other words, feel other passions, have
nor figure, appearance, disposition, tissue
the same?
>To be in different states without a change
>is not a possibility

We can be precise. The factors are
in the animal and/or the machine the factors are
communication and/or control, both involve
the message. And what is the message? The message is
a discrete or continuous sequence of measurable events distributed in time

is the birth of air, is
the birth of water, is

a state between
the origin and
the end, between
birth and the beginning of
another fetid nest

is change, presents
no more than itself

And the too strong grasping of it,
when it is pressed together and condensed,
loses it

This very thing you are

II

They buried their dead in a sitting posture
serpent   cane   razor   ray of the sun

And she sprinkled water on the head of the child, crying
"Cioa-coatl! Cioa-coatl!"
with her face to the west

Where the bones are found, in each personal heap
with what each enjoyed, there is always
the Mongolian louse

The light is in the east. Yes. And we must rise, act. Yet
in the west, despite the apparent darkness (the whiteness
which covers all), if you look, if you can bear, if you can, long enough

as long as it was necessary for him, my guide
to look into the yellow of that longest-lasting rose

so you must, and, in that whiteness, into that face, with what candor, look

and, considering the dryness of the place
the long absence of an adequate race

(of the two who first came, each a conquistador, one healed, the other
tore the eastern idols down, toppled
the temple walls, which, says the excuser
were black from human gore)

hear
hear, where the dry blood talks
    where the old appetite walks

                    la piu saporita et migliore
                    che si possa truovar al mondo

where it hides, look
in the eye how it runs
in the flesh / chalk

      but under these petals
      in the emptiness
      regard the light, contemplate
      the flower

whence it arose

      with what violence benevolence is bought
      what cost in gesture justice brings
      what wrongs domestic rights involve
      what stalks
      this silence

what pudor pejorocracy affronts
how awe, night-rest and neighborhood can rot
what breeds where dirtiness is law
what crawls
below

III
    I am no Greek, hath not th'advantage.
    And of course, no Roman :

he can take no risk that matters,
the risk of beauty least of all.

But I have my kin, if for no other reason than
(as he said, next of kin) I commit myself, and,
given my freedom, I'd be a cad
if I didn't. Which is most true.

It works out this way, despite the disadvantage.
I offer, in explanation, a quote:
si j'ai du goût, ce n'est guères
que pour la terre et les pierres

Despite the discrepancy (an   ocean   courage   age)
this is also true: if I have any taste
it is only because I have interested myself
in what was slain in the sun

     I pose you your question:

shall you uncover honey / where maggots are?

     I hunt among stones

So. It is there. The poem stands in itself. Sherman Paul's
gloss of the poem tells us much of what it means but I am more
impressed with the poem than with what it means. I am more
impressed with an ocelot when it is in front of me than with
the history of the ocelot. The ocelot means itself, and it means,
to me, the perceptions that it creates in me. I am more im-
pressed with the huge black and white calligraphic paintings
of Franz Kline and what they create in my physiomental sky-
field, with their transmission of energy, than I am with what
Kline specifically meant.

This is not to reduce projective verse to a nonintellective cave-man poetry. (Anyway, let's remember that the Cro-Magnon brain was considerably larger than ours and that we are his self-domesticated, mentally scaled-down children.) Our simplistic society is represented by Pop Art. It turns away from elegance toward modularly repeated and machine-made repetitive particles such as the soup can, byte, xerox duplicate, and tenement condo. On the other hand, energy poems are like dreams and fairy tales—they are compressions of many aspects of experience simultaneously. They are unique, special, not easy. Each is a new construct in a storm of newly invented structures that the poet creates.

A projective "ode" like *The Kingfishers* may stand as something has never stood before; not only is it unique in its energy and meaning, it may also figure as an ideogram. It is made up of separate and sometimes logically incomplete references, which, put together, all mean one new thing. It also calls to mind an Amerindian medicine bundle—powers are put together in a new way and their purpose is to bring changes into the universe. Obviously *The Kingfishers* is personal; possibly it is primitive; and certainly it is sophisticated. Beyond that it may be titanic—it may be using the powers of the mindbody in a new way and be beyond the postmodern. *Postmodern* is, after all, only a reflection of limited aspects of an old, large, powerful medicine bundle.

Two writers come to mind: Shelley, writing his ode *Mont Blanc* in the vale of Chamouni while looking up at the Swiss mountain; Jack Kerouac, writing, occasionally under the influence of morphine, in Mexico City in his great mumbling, lucid, jazzlike, visionary, singing poem *Mexico City Blues*. Shelley's poem begins:

Mont Blanc

The everlasting universe of things
Flows through the mind, and rolls its rapid waves,
Now dark—now glittering—now reflecting gloom—
Now lending splendour, where from secret springs
The source of human thought its tribute brings
Of waters,—with a sound but half its own,
Such as a feeble brook will oft assume
In the wild woods, among the mountains lone,
Where waterfalls around it leap for ever,
Where woods and winds contend, and a vast river
Over its rocks ceaselessly bursts and raves.

In that energy structure Shelley allows his intellect—at its highest capacity—stimulated by conversations with Mary, Byron, and their entourage, to become a system through which energy passes to organize the system. In the process of almost onomatopoetically recreating the wild mountain scene in the music of the poem, Shelley creates a new poem shape. In it he may, in fact, be the voice of the universe that has broken through his person to sing itself in a previously unexpressed way. The poem may be a complex molecule of perception. He continues:

Thus thou, Ravine of Arve—dark, deep Ravine—
Thou many-coloured, many-voicèd vale,
Over whose pines, and crags, and caverns sail
Fast cloud-shadows and sunbeams: awful scene,
Where Power in likeness of the Arve comes down
From the ice-gulfs that gird his secret throne,
Bursting through these dark mountains like the flame

Of lightning through the tempest;—thou dost lie,
Thy giant brood of pines around thee clinging,
Children of elder time, in whose devotion
The chainless winds still come and ever came
To drink their odours, and their mighty swinging
To hear—an old and solemn harmony;
Thine earthly rainbows stretched across the sweep
Of the aethereal waterfall, whose veil
Robes some unsculptured image; the strange sleep
Which when the voices of the desert fail
Wraps all in its own deep eternity;—
Thy caverns echoing to the Arve's commotion,
A loud, lone sound no other sound can tame;
Thou art pervaded with that ceaseless motion,
Thou art the path of that unresting sound—
Dizzy Ravine! and when I gaze on thee
I seem as in a trance sublime and strange
To muse on my own separate fantasy.

These lines seem to be the energy of the universe expressing itself upon the complex organism of Shelley's body as if he were a typewriter of protein spirit. It is the river below and the glacier above in their immediate energy forms—and the clouds passing over—and the movement of storms over the peaks—and the burst of pines from the dark subsoil into the vivid air—that are the most present charges. It seems that way, for that is what Shelley paints with his sensorium and sense of music. But there is also an older, deeper energy source present. Beneath the mammal-human biography of Shelley's life there is a very ancient consciousness expressing itself in his imagination—as his imagination is liberated by the inspiration of his surroundings.

Many billions of years before the present all the physical matter in the universe exploded (goes one story) from a single

superdense ball. The turbulence of the exploded matter, drift-
ing through the space that it seems to have created, was not
evenly spread and densifications of matter took place in cer-
tain areas of space. The densifications became complex and
compact and they in turn exploded; the product of the explo-
sion was the original, simple material, plus new assemblies of
that material, which were more complex. As these expanded
through new space, and previously created space, there were
further densifications of both complex and old material—and
probably more explosions and the creation of yet more com-
plex matter out of the simpler materials. This matter densified
into galaxies of stars. Then planets densified in place around
stars. Because of the Ur-ancient energy of the very first explo-
sion, which still operated in more and more complex manners,
reconcentrated energy streamed from the stars across the sur-
face of this planet. The surface of Earth complicated itself into
very new molecules which in turn took miraculous shapes.
These then crumpled themselves for their own preservation
and the extension of energy. They created a negentropic danc-
ing film that a biologist friend calls "rainbow mud"—of which
we are a part—of which Shelley was a part. The material of
Shelley was in the original primeval explosion and went through
all the densifications and expansions and complications.
Then, in 1816, the material of the universe in a point of novel
self-comprehension (as all points are novel) stood in the stance
of poetry admiring itself from primeval past to most modern
retreating glacier and roaring river—and naturally played
upon itself and sang.

Small wonder that William Carlos Williams believed that
poetry is in *things*—that there is poetry in a wheelbarrow
glazed with rain.

Shelley continues in the poem:

I seem as in a trance sublime and strange
To muse on my own separate fantasy,
My own, my human mind, which passively
Now renders and receives fast influencings,
Holding an unremitting interchange
With the clear universe of things around;
One legion of wild thoughts, whose wandering wings
Now float above thy darkness, and now rest
Where that or thou art no unbidden guest,
In the still cave of the witch Poesy,
Seeking among the shadows that pass by
Ghost of all things that are, some shade of thee,
Some phantom, some faint image; till the breast
From which they fled recalls them, thou art there!

It is possible that in all art we remember WHO WE ARE—
and also celebrate *who we are.* One of Kerouac's biographers,
Gerry Nicosia, informs us that in 1958 Olson called Kerouac
"a great poet." It is not surprising that Olson, as well as the
Beats and the San Francisco poets, was able to recognize Ker-
ouac so clearly so quickly. Energy in poetry was important to
all.

Kerouac is being popularized as an icon of culture—my re-
gret is that sight of him as an artist will be lost. We'll know his
name and some work considered typical. But we'll miss one of
the finest, brightest sensoriums that has graced verse with in-
telligence and intellect. This has already happened to D.H.
Lawrence. Lawrence is now known as a novelist—and remem-
bered for his more novelistic novels. Lawrence's greatest gifts
were as a poet—in poems of love, birds, beasts, and flowers—
and in his essays of place and of physiological insight and psy-
chophysiological processes. To read the poem *Bavarian Gen-*

tians or the extended essay *Fantasia of the Unconscious* is to know the bright creature who trembles behind the costumed facade of the novels.

Similarly, Kerouac is best known for his novel *On the Road,* but his masterpiece is *Mexico City Blues,* a religious poem startling in its majesty and comedy and gentleness and vision.

Kerouac is known worldwide as a novelist. He is sometimes also known as the writer of haiku-type poems or intermediate-length poems on the subject of Rimbaud or Buddhism. But Kerouac is little known as the author of several major poems which he considered to be blues works. These books include the unpublished *Washington D.C. Blues, San Francisco Blues,* and *Berkeley Blues.* They range in style from Dos Passos-like descriptive verse to poetrylike journals. Outstanding in all modern poetry is the epic-length *Mexico City Blues.* Kerouac's note on the front of the published edition says:

I want to be considered a jazz poet blowing a long blues in an afternoon jam session on Sunday. I take 242 choruses; my ideas vary and sometimes roll from chorus to chorus or from halfway through a chorus to halfway into the next.

The rules of *Mexico City Blues* were that they should be written on the pages of a pocket notebook such as Kerouac nearly always carried. Each page of the notebook would be a chorus. Eventually, in the developing structure of the poem, each line becomes a complete, and whole, independent image. As in the 230th Chorus:

Love's multitudinous boneyard
    of decay,
The spilled milk of heroes,
Destruction of silk kerchiefs
    by dust storm,

Caress of heroes blindfolded to posts,
Murder victims admitted to this life,
Skeletons bartering fingers and joints . . .

A further rule of *Mexico City Blues* was that it must all be spontaneous—all a risk—a free, inspired, or noninspired, flowing statement, liberated from judgments about its value. It was to be done for itself—as an organism lives for itself.

In the early fifties, when Kerouac began the poem in Mexico City, he had recently read and been impressed by Ezra Pound's *Cantos*. There is no doubt Kerouac wanted to emulate the experience of writing the *Cantos* and create his own equivalent work. He had been evolving ideas of a spontaneous bop prosody and apparently he simply began to let the poem flow like bop (not that bop is simple). He was writing voices he had overheard into the bodies of the choruses and he was writing the structure of his passing thoughts. He approached the idea of Sunyatta—of Nothingness Buddhism—and of our ignorance of it.

1st Chorus

Butte Magic of Ignorance
Butte Magic
Is the same as no-Butte
            All one light
            Old Rough Roads
            One High Iron
            Mainway

            Denver is the same
"The guy I was with his uncle was

the governor of Wyoming"
  "Course he paid me back"
  Ten Days
    Two Weeks
      Stock and Joint

"Was an old crook anyway"

The same voice on the same ship
The Supreme Vehicle
      S.S. Excalibur
      Maynard
      Mainline
      Mountain
      Merudvhaga
        Mersion of Missy

2nd Chorus

Man is not worried in the middle

Man in the Middle
Is not Worried
He knows his Karma
Is not buried

But his Karma,
Unknown to him,
May end—

Which is Nirvana

Wild men
Who kill
Have Karmas
Of ill

Good men
Who love
Have Karmas
Of dove

Snakes are Poor Denizens of Hell
Have come surreptitioning
Through the tall grass
To face the pool of clear frogs

So it is to be a Buddhist poem—a "Mersion of Missy," as he tells us in the first chorus—about karma and liberation.

Thus, he begins simply—almost effortlessly—an easy chorus, but one which shows a master ear and master skill carrying over from earlier complex works in prose and verse. As the choruses continue through clouds of morphine, and overhearings, and spontaneous expressions, and perceptions, and word games, and insights into Buddhism, they focus on the retelling of his long-dead brother Gerard's mystical visions preceding his early death. As Kerouac's cool mind, hand, and ear extend the poem it becomes the channel for great energy. There is a mammalian, powerful force moving through the soft lines of the poem as it flows from dippy to beatific as it extends itself. Kerouac is tremendously involved in his emotions about Gerard. That emotional involvement begins to power the already flowing choruses. The energy moving through the systemless system acts to organize the system with its own self-invented rules. In our Euro-American universe of discourse we believe that if something is *serious* it is witnessably big and gloomy—and realistic. Kerouac made joking reference to "big serious gloomy poets"—poking at the rigid cant of literary self-investment. Kerouac was writing a big, serious poem, but it was not gloomy overall; it was not realistic; and it smiled at itself and laughed at the world outrageously. The poem is like ourselves at our unchained moments when we are able to move from our established self-investments and stride on new stepping-stones to a point of risk, growth, change, or maturity. Kerouac was writing a mystical (in its hope), anarchist, epic-length, and open-ended poem.

This great self-organizing act of verse-energy as it flows on and on, becoming more diverse, stronger in its self-supporting complexity—like the systems described by H. T. Odum in his remarkable *Environment, Power and Society*—begins to create a fundament that never existed before. The beautifully controlled energy of the poem—like the serene energy of Mark Rothko in his contemplative canvases—creates a substrate—creates a new world, place, ground, or nourishing energy, in which a vision may come into being. A similar thing happened when I wrote my long poem *Dark Brown*—when I believed the poem had ended I found, instead, that I had laid back the space, as if I were stepping into a cave behind a waterfall, and in the space a liberating sexual ode appeared. When the ode was written, another sexual vision appeared in the base it had created. I began to understand that there is never a final mystery—there is always a quark within the quark—always a structure reflecting itself in Indra's net.

In Kerouac's *Mexico City Blues* a self-created substrate—a surpassing religious vision was born—or was blown, as one blows a saxophone! It is the surpassing religious visionary poetic statement of the twentieth century.

211th Chorus

The wheel of the quivering meat
                          conception
Turns in the void expelling human beings,
Pigs, turtles, frogs, insects, nits,
Mice, lice, lizards, rats, roan,
Racinghorses, poxy bucolic pigtics,
Horrible unnameable lice of vultures,
Murderous attacking dog-armies
of Africa, Rhinos roaming in the
                          jungle,
Vast boars and huge gigantic bull
Elephants, rams, eagles, condors,
Pones and Porcupines and Pills—
All the endless conception of living
                          beings
Gnashing everywhere in Consciousness
Throughout the ten directions of space
Occupying all the quarters in & out,
From supermicroscopic no-bug
To huge Galaxy Lightyear Bowell
Illuminating the sky of one Mind—
        Poor! I wish I was free
        of that slaving meat wheel
        and safe in heaven dead

212th Chorus

All of this meat is in dreadful pain
Anytime circumstances attain
To its attention like a servant
And pricking goads invest the flesh,
And it quivers, meat, & owner cries
And wishes "Why was I born with a body,
Why do I have this painful hive

Of hope-of-honey-milk yet bane
Of bitterest reward, as if, to wish
For flesh was sin alone itself—?"
And now you gotta pay, rhinoceros
                             and you,
    Tho his hide's toughern ten young men
Armed with picks against the Grim
                             Reaper
Whose scythe is preceded by pitchforks
Of temptation & hell, the Horror:
    "Think of pain, you're being hurt,
    Hurry, hurry, think of pain
    Before they make a fool of you
    And discover that you dont feel
    It's the best possible privilege
    To be alive just to die
    And die in denizen of misery"

227th Chorus

Merde and misery,
I'm completely in pain
Waiting without mercy
For the worst to happen.
I'm completely at a loss,
        There is no hope
Though I know the arbitrary conception
    of suffering is racking
    my metaphysical
    handicapped ribs,
    and I dont even exist less sing,
    and I been paid
    for work I done
    when I was young
    and work was fun
    and I dont know name from mercy,
    aint got no blues

no shoes no eyes
no shoetongues, lungs,
no happiness, no art
nothing to do, nothin to part,
no hairs to split
sidewalks to spit,
words to make flit
in the fun-of make-it,
      horror & makeshift poetry
      covering the fact I'm afraid
      to work at a steady job
jungles of hair on my wrists
magnified 1000 times
      in Hells of Eternity

228th Chorus

Praised be man, he is existing in milk
      and living in lilies—
And his violin music takes place in milk
      and creamy emptiness—
Praised be the unfolded inside petal
      flesh of tend'rest thought—
      (petrels on the follying
      wave-valleys idly
      sing themselves asleep)—
Praised be delusion, the ripple—
Praised the Holy Ocean of Eternity—
Praised be I, writing, dead already &
      dead again—
  Dipped in ancid inkl
        the flamd
        of T i m
  the Anglo Oglo Saxon Maneuvers
Of Old Poet-o's—
      Praised be wood, it is milk—
      Praised be Honey at the Source—

Praised be the embrace of soft sleep
—the valor of angels in valleys
   of hell on earth below—
Praised be the Non ending—
Praised be the lights of earth-man—
Praised be the watchers—
     Praised be my fellow man
     For dwelling in milk

229th Chorus

In the ocean there's a very sad turtle
(Even tho the SS *Mainline* Fishin Ship
     is reeling in the merit like mad)
Swims longmouthed & sad, looking
     for the Impossible Except Once
     afternoon when the Yoke, Oh,
     the old Buddha Yoke set a-floatin
     is in the water where the turtle raises
     his be-watery snop to the sea
     and the Yoke yokes the Turtle
       a Eternity—
"Tell me O Bhikkus,
     what are the chances,
       of such a happening,
         for the turtle is old
           and the yoke free,
           and the 7 oceans bigger
             than any we see
             in this tiny party."
Chances are slender—
     In a million million billion kotis
     of Aeons and Incalculables, Yes,
     the Turtle will set that Yoke free,
     but till then, harder yet
     are the chances, for a man
     to be reborn a man
     in this Karma earth

230th Chorus

Love's multitudinous boneyard
    of decay,
The spilled milk of heroes,
Destruction of silk kerchiefs
    by dust storm,
Caress of heroes blindfolded to posts,
Murder victims admitted to this life,
Skeletons bartering fingers and joints,
The quivering meat of the elephants of kindness
    being torn apart by vultures,
Conceptions of delicate kneecaps,
Fear of rats dripping with bacteria,
Golgotha Cold Hope for Gold Hope,
Damp leaves of Autumn against
    the wood of boats,
Seahorse's delicate imagery of glue,
Sentimental "I Love You" no more,
Death by long exposure to defilement,
Frightening ravishing mysterious beings
    concealing their sex,
Pieces of the Buddha-material frozen
    and sliced microscopically
In Morgues of the North,
Penis apples going to seed,
The severed gullets more numerous than sands—
        Like kissing my kitten in the belly
        the softness of our reward

    Kerouac not only presents his Mahayana, Hua-yen vision of the interdependency of the phantasmic illusion of Maya, he also shows us that even our art of poetry is illusion.

    While we are here, in illusion, let us regale ourselves in it. It is only by seeing the complexity of our selves that we can sense the complexity of the illusion. It may be that only after experiencing the consciousness of the physicality of matter may we see if there is something beyond the veil.

Shelley said in his memorable sonnet:

Lift not the painted veil which those who live
Call Life: though unreal shapes be pictured there,
And it but mimic all we would believe . . .

And of course his admonition *not to lift* was in fact an encouragement to lift the veil. Our joy is in our animal selves and in the consciousness that is the flesh. Surely that is the way into the poem.

In the late fifties, while corresponding with Olson and developing my own projective verse, I wrote *Rant Block*. The beginning of the poem will end this section and begin the next, "Breakthrough."

RANT BLOCK

THERE IS NO FORM BUT SHAPE! NO LOGIC BUT SEQUENCE!
SHAPE the cloak and being of love, desire, hatred,
hunger. BULK or BODY OF WHAT WE ARE AND STRIVE
FOR. ((OR
there is a series of synaptic
stars. Lines of them. It's that simple
or brutal. And, worst, they
become blurred.

2.

Breakthrough

Nature reaches its most appealing manifestations of beauty, intricacy, and mystery in the very complex systems: the tropical coral reef, the tropical rain forest, the benthos-dominated marine systems on the west coasts of continents of temperate zones, the bottom of the deep sea, and some ancient lakes of Africa. These places are environmentally stable, and the species networks that develop there have great specialization and division of labor in the same way that the city of New York has enormous diversity of occupations. Complex networks must maintain controls for stability, but there is energy for control because the environments are initially stable, requiring no great energy drains for physiological adaptation.

from "Complex and Beautiful Systems"
found in *Environment, Power, and Society*
Howard T. Odum

Thus a system can evolve new patterns more rapidly when there are more power flows, providing excess quantities of choice in the form of extra offspring, more specialized mechanisms for selecting, and more reward cycling. Without power, excess change in the direction of new order is at times impossible, although loss of structure is possible.

from "Power Cost of Evolution"
found in *Environment, Power, and Society*
Howard T. Odum

New species are formed when new adaptations receive better loop reinforcement and reward from the system in which speciation is occurring. For reinforcement the direction of the adaptive change must be toward greater energy flow through the population circuit. Adaptations that tend to circumvent system-limiting factors and increase flow are rewarded by the feedback loops. In this way species are developed for the compatibility of systems.

from "Speciation and Insulation"
found in *Environment, Power, and Society*
Howard T. Odum

In the fifties Robert Creeley reminded me of Olson's maxim that form is the extension of content. I felt that this was the complement to Olson's reassertion of Edward Dahlberg's dictum that one perception must follow instanter upon another. I found difficulty, however, with the word *form*. In essence Creeley was correct that form is an extension of content, but I could not use this concept of *form* in my work. Even when *form* was redefined as an extension of content it still carried limitations.

As I worked with plays and essays, I found a writhing multidimensionality of thought. As my knowledge of biology expanded I was not content with critical descriptions and analyses of literature. They were confined to reason and logic. Yet reason and logic, in their usual manifestations, create a veneer over potent forces that are not yet faced in the art of Poetry.

When I was studying Olson's poetry a poem grew in my notebooks as I have heard that some Beethoven compositions grew: a line would occur—I'd try it with other lines—more would accrue to it. I would take a section and then more would be added and discarded. At the end, rather than a tortured and studied poem, it felt like my most sudden thought. I had carved through to reach spontaneous thought and to let it speak as it might if it had been written spontaneously.

Rant Block, the opening lines of which closed the preceding section, felt like a new breakthrough:

85

RANT BLOCK

THERE IS NO FORM BUT SHAPE! NO LOGIC BUT SEQUENCE!
SHAPE the cloak and being of love, desire, hatred,
hunger. BULK or BODY OF WHAT WE ARE AND STRIVE
FOR. ((OR
there is a series of synaptic
stars. Lines of them. It's that simple
or brutal. And, worst, they
become blurred.

SNOUT EYES
As negative as beauty is.))
LEVIATHAN WE SWOOP DOWN AND COVER
what is ours. Desires
OR BLOCK THEM. SICKNESS—ACHES.
Are heroes in simplicity with open eyes
and hungers. Truth
does not hurt us. Is more difficult than
beauty is. We smolder smoke pours
from our ears in stopping what we feel.
(free air)
Your hand, by your side, is never love.

FORM IS AN EVASION! POETRY
A PATTERN TO BE FILLED BY FAGGOTS.

WILD ANGER MORE THAN CULTIVATED LOVE!!
Wolf and salmon shapes free to kill
for food love and hatred.
Life twists its head *from side to side* to test
the elements and seek
for breath and meat to feed on.
I AM A FIRE AND I MOVE IN AN INFERNO
sick I smolder
and do not burn clear.

Smoldering makes nets of smoke upon the world.
I am clean free and radiant and beauty follows this.
Not first but follows.
What is love or hatred but a voice I hear
of what I see and touch. Who is the man
within that moves me that I never see
but hear and speak to? Who are you
to stop me? Why are you here
to block me? All I choose to see
is beauty. Nerves. Inferno!
Fakery of emotions. Desire for presumption. Love of glory. Pride.
Vanity. Dead and unfilled desires. Regrets. Tired arms. Tables. Lies.
BLOOD AND MUSCLE BLOOD AND MUSCLE BLOOD AND
                              [MUSCLE BLOOD AND MUSCLE
Calling pure love lust to block myself and die with that upon my head?
Wit and false stupidity with no point to it but the most tangled ends
unwitnessed by myself in fulfillment. When I found you sleeping
why didn't I? Would you love me for it? Do I care? OH. And smoke.
AND NOT THAT FINE SWING
of wing or fin!

And never chivalry. The strive to rise. The act of grace. Of self.
Of sureness large enough for generosity. The overflowing.
But the chiding carping voice and action. What is this? Why
DON'T WE KICK IN THE WALLS? KICK IN THE WALLS!
INVENT OURSELVES IN IMAGES OF WHAT WE FEEL.

WHERE HAVE ALL THESE CLOUDS OF SMOKE COME FROM?
I am the animal seraph that I know I am!

And I burn with fine pure love and fire, electricity and oxygen
a thing of protein and desire,   !!
and all of this is ugliness
and talk not freedom
OH SHIT HELL FUCK THAT WE ARE BLOCKED
in striving by what we hate
surrounding us. And do not break it in our strike

at it. The part of us
so trained to live in filth and never stir.
THAT I WAIT FOR YOU TO RAISE YOUR HAND FIRST
(to me)
This is sickness. This is what
I hate within
myself. This
is the war I battle in. This is the neverending instant.
The black hour that never ceases. This is the darkness about
the burning.
The form and talk of form as if flames obeyed without
dwindling.

These are the dull words from an animal of real flesh. Why?
Where is the fire in them?
Never let them stop until they are
moving things. Until
they stir the fire!
Never let them stand stemmed by form again. Let
my face be radiant and give off light!
Never allow sign of love where hatred dwells!

If there are bastions, let my love be walls!

The concept of form needed statement in a new way. I told
that to Allen Ginsberg and he proposed that *Art is shapely,
mind is shapely.* But I found myself intent upon shape and not
necessarily upon what is shapely. I believed, also, that it was
not appropriate to continue the Descartian division of mind
and physiology.

Diogenes, the Groucho Marx of philosophy, said: *I have
seen Plato's cup and his table but I have not seen his cupness
and his tableness.*

It was time to look at the cups and tables—and the body. The mind is inseparable from the body and too much energy has been spent looking at the mind (whether shapely or not) of poetry, and not enough at the body. Similarly, the structure of poetry had been often looked at (though not clearly), but such structure had never been looked at as an extension of physiology. Certainly it had not been viewed in the light of physiology being an extension of phylogeny.

In *Rant Block* I made the discovery that "THERE IS NO FORM BUT SHAPE! NO LOGIC BUT SEQUENCE!" and the discovery that shape is the cloak, and simultaneously the being, the actual organism of love, desire, hatred, and hunger. I saw the Bulk, and the Bulk is the Body of what we are and what we strive for . . . I felt that our lives were lines of synaptic stars—literally—and it seemed *that* simple—and it is—and *that* brutal. It is life, not beauty, that we are after, for if there is beauty (and we do live in beauty) it is our perceptions raining lightning upon our fleshly pads that is glorious.

I felt the poem *Rant Block* begin to come to life and become a breakthrough. I had considered my poems to be extensions of myself as much as my hand or arm are extensions of me. Now it occurred to me that a poem could even become a living bio-alchemical organism. I knew it was preposterous but then, so is much of art. It is *almost* unbelievable that Dante walked through the Inferno with Virgil.

I believed that *Rant Block* began to tug and pull and move like an organism—that like a wolf or salmon it could turn its head from side to side to test the elements and seek for breath. I wanted to write a poem that would come to life and be a living organism.

Ernst Haeckel, an advanced biological thinker at the turn of the century, was a disciple of Goethe and Darwin and a visionary artist of radiolarians and nudibranchs (brightly colored

molluscs that fly through tidepools like butterflies). He coined the word *ecology* (*oikos* plus *logy—house* and *study-of*). Haeckel also conceived the proposal: Ontogeny recapitulates phylogeny. Haeckel meant that the individual, in his growth from meeting of sperm and ovum at conception, lives out, in foetus, the growth and evolution of his tribe: that first he is an amoeba, then a colonial organism, then an invertebrate, then a lancet, then a fish, until at last he is a mammal and a human.

The action poem can no more help telling us about the acting writer than the action painting can exist without our wonder at the painter's markings on the canvas. We see this in the loops of Pollock's dripped, *duende*like blue, purple, red, and silver, as strands pile over one another. We are given information in contemplating, or remembering, the quiet, huge patches of green and purple upon scarlet that Rothko floats over his surfaces in washes of pigment. *Information is knowledge that effects the future.*

To understand action poems, or action painting, or action music, or the public and private events of our active lives, it is helpful to understand the nature of energy in biological systems.

Blake said that energy is eternal delight.

The *Oxford English Dictionary* describes the etymology of energy from the late Latin *energia*, originally from the Greek ενεργεσ, which comes from εν + εργον (*en* + *ergon*—work). Example one states: *With reference to speech or writing: force or vigour of expression.* The second example: *Exercise of power, actual working, operation, activity; freq. in philosophical language.*

Blake's proposal is rich because it speaks of energy not as a part of discourse but as a power in use, which we perceive: eternal delight.

The first *O.E.D.* example tells us what is missing in most writing—"Force or vigour of expression." In looking at energy in organisms and art it is valuable to study the relationship of energy to information, and to memory, and to diversity, and to organization, and to complexity.

It is not easy to see energy in use. To see energy in action in the bundles and bodies that contain it, it is useful to turn to Ramon Margalef's *Perspectives in Ecological Theory* and especially to the section: "The Ecosystem as a Cybernetic System." It is in such frontier work as Margalef's that we are the closest to a description of the systemless system of negentropy, that is, in fact, defined by the presence and nature of life.

First, it is necessary to point out that complex systems are more stable through time than simpler systems. A system that has within it loops of energy and feedback and processing and reprocessing resembles a bridge with many support systems balancing out gravity's pull. It is like a building with internal walls and pillars and exterior flying buttresses. Evolved, informed complexity and diversity within the system allows the possibility of its extension through time. For instance, in government we have bureaucracies. They are clearly foolish wastes but in the long run they are stabilizers of the governing system. They slow down, complicate, and solidify it. Vertebrates have complicated glandular, venous, and nervous systems that are not necessary to the higher invertebrates—but the individual vertebrate is a more stable system than a mollusc, and will probably live and produce longer.

Kerouac's huge, self-forming system of *Mexico City Blues* is a much more stable system than sheer, shapeless automatic writing. It begins to become an organism. Olson's *Maximus Poems* through its obsessive complication of meanings becomes both so daring and so stable that the last volume could be pieced together and completed as a semistochastic, monumental collage by Olson's executor, George Butterick. It works! It works and it takes away the breath and it is stable because it is complex. Yet it looks anachronistic to those who are more and more simplified by their relationships to a modular, electronic, mechanical world. It is mind-boggling to those who forget their ancestors were Cro-Magnons, to those who forget the bison on the cave walls and the old magic of individual imagination.

In his section "The Ecosystem as a Cybernetic System," Margalef has a passage entitled "A Basic Principle of Organization."

Everywhere in nature we can draw arbitrary surfaces and arbitrarily declare them boundaries separating two subsystems. More often than not it turns out that such boundaries are asymmetric; they separate two subsystems that, although arbitrarily limited, are different in their degrees of organization. There is some energy exchange between the two subsystems in the sense that the less-organized subsystem gives energy to the more-organized, and, in the process of exchange, some information in the less-organized is destroyed and some information is gained by the already more-organized.

What Margalef is saying goes against the morals of the universe of discourse. However, it is not cynical—nor Machiavellian. It is simply an observation. Beautiful if true. It is one of the wellsprings of exuberance. Blake said, "Exuberance is Beauty" and "Energy is Eternal Delight." He also said, "The Tygers of Wrath are wiser than the Horses of Instruction." Our system is the Tyger of delighted wrath, and the other, the prey system, is the horse of aspiring instruction. Margalef continues, "Probably it is useful . . . to remember a few such couplings"—and he gives examples of numerous systems in nature and society:

gas / Maxwell demon, electrical conductor / semiconductor, atmosphere / sea, environment / thermostat, substrate / enzyme, enzyme / RNA, cytoplasm / nucleus, mesenchym / nervous system, biotope / community, plants / animals, prey / predator, plankton / benthos, agrarian communities / industrial societies.

In all such examples, the second subsystem experiences more predictable changes through time. In so doing it stores information better and is a more efficient information channel. The first subsystem is subject to a stronger energy flow and, in fact, the second system feeds on the surplus of such energy.

This is an image of the universe. Life recapitulates the processes of matter. Densified areas of greater organization react with nebulous matter in space and are informed by it. There is further densification. It reaches climax. It explodes—the material retains certain pieces of information and gains more organization in the explosion—and so forth. Margalef continues:

It is a basic property of nature, from the point of view of cybernetics, that any exchange between two systems of different information content does not result in a partition or equalizing of the information, but increases the difference. The system with more accumulated information becomes still richer from the exchange.

This statement is a truth that we usually state unhappily, as if it were unpleasant—though there is no reason why we cannot rejoice in it, since it is the principle in the streaming of cytoplasm and the evolution of life. All lives and pleasures are made possible by it.

Broadly speaking, the same principle is valid for persons and human organizations; any exchange increases to a greater extent the information of the party already better informed. Here it is pertinent to give to the concept of information the meaning of something which is arrived at by a succession of decisions and which influences the future.

Now Margalef comes to his image, though it is so generalized that we will, at the very best, see it as an abstraction. Still, it is powerful if it can be seen.

The unit in such information exchanges is an event taking place between two elements A and B. Suppose element A has a more indeterminate position and a less predictable future, its position being associated with a more diffuse cloud of probabilities. Such an element carries and can give off more energy. Element B has opposite properties. The interaction event must occur closer to B than to A, and the memory of element A will be annihilated in the interaction. If there is an increase of information content, it will accrue to B. Decision-making means friction, and the bill is footed mostly by A.

One can picture element A as a jumping, dispersed cloud of energy and potentialities. B, on the other hand, can be seen as a circular sawblade-shaped, complex system that is slowly and steadily rotating. As A comes within the field of B, due to its less informed movements, it is cut into by B, and part of the structure of A is taken into and feeds B.

Margalef concludes this section:

Such relations are compounded in a hierarchical organization and are reflected at every level. Any organization can be analyzed by dissecting it into smaller and smaller blocks; the pattern of the whole organization is reflected at every division in differences of organization on either side of the boundary and in the exchange of energy at each level. Such analysis frees us from the need to define ecosystems that are more or less closed.

In the early seventies, the thinking of H. T. Odum, of Harold Morowitz in biophysics, and of Margalef in ecological systems did much to clarify my unorganized perceptions of the fifties and sixties.

Energy—or its use—*does* evolve. It is not a bouncing, wild-eyed jitterbug full of undirectable, diffuse energy that writes the projective poem. The projective poem must come from a powerful, complex, informed—ultimately stable substrate; from a mind/body in physiological training, in resonance with an evolving systemless system. Olson, Snyder, Creeley, Duncan, Kerouac, Ginsberg, Whalen are all men with large, complex personalities. Their energies, as manifested in structure and exuberance, are self-contained. Lord Byron for all of his rampaging was enormously stable in his creative person.

Artists develop the containment of complex energy as they mature. They feed from the energy of the substrate around them as it informs their senses. It is an organic process; it has no other rules than the rules of sigh and cry and of movement and of growth.

The poem *Rant Block* was a breakthrough because it went through the crust of the verbal universe for a sea lion swim in the world of physiology. The poem had been informed—in formed—made into a shape with possibility of life through my studies of biology and the essays I wrote on the subject of the body-meaning of "Revolt." *Rant Block* was floating on the field of studies. It came from field work. Snyder's work was built upon, and grew with his work in forests, and on the ocean, and in oil tankers, and in studies of Zen—not only Zen from books but from practice in a Japanese monastery. Duncan's work grew out of his physical wrestling with the literature he loved—with his teaching, and speaking, and experimenting and its related states of consciousness, and from his dance of inspiration. Ginsberg grew from his immersion in the study of the consciousness of himself and friends, and altered states of consciousness, and the great labor of endless, idealistic, self-shaping writing.

Everyone is always ready to go from the field into the theatre of their expression. It is one and the same.

*   *   *

Corresponding with Olson in 1957 or 1958, I wrote a letter that was primarily about the experience of the peyote high. It began with a quote from Olson's own essay, "Human Universe."

Charles,

A fantastic thing. "The admission these people give me and one another is direct, and the individual who peers out from that flesh is precisely himself, is a curious wandering animal like me—" etc. Peyote is mentioned once or twice in *Maximus*—have you eaten it? You said *Peyote bean* (a joke?) or is there also a Peyote bean? Ah well anyway:

I have taken Peyote now and your *Human Universe* is *more* true—which I would have thought to be impossible. I wish I hadn't been so boxed when you gave your lectures in San Francisco. With the peyote I came to realize—came to realize HAH, I KNEW, know, that we are absolute individual animals. Looking out at objects on a table, I saw that they were as unique and singular as a cactus on a bare desert and in that same stasis that matter has come to our senses. Of course, also, they were with form, shape, color and those were much more intense. That is, the objects were *themselves*. Themselves. Whatever they were, sugarbowl, coffe pot, spoon. I am only using the table as an example—a microcosm—the whole physical universe is that way.

Here is the way I see it. Peyote puts you back within your own skin into the Human Universe. Into your own personal, animal, individual universe. And you look out into the physical universe and see it as *only* the physical universe—all those emotional drags of unimportance are gone. I mean the emotional drags that you project but do not handle within yourself or only off the top of yourself.

Viz.,

Sugarbowl—I do not like it because my mother gave it to me. Also, once I thought it was pretty but now it is ugly to me. It contains sugar—the price of sugar I note has gone up—I'm broke this week. etc., etc. to the infinite.

Coffeepot—all of the emotional reactions to and against coffee and coffee pots, etc.

Spoon—the same as above.

Those are the reactions of the down state. And what do they have
to do with individuality? Nothing anyway to do with that individ-
ual within the skin who looks out of the eyes. All of the above are
projections forming a web that is a part of that process of *classifica-
tion*. (When it comes to getting the right word here I am not good at
it since I know no philosophy.) I realized, later, after the main high
was over, that these emotional projections that are not part of the
central individuality and Human Universe actually do form webs
around each object so that we do not see them as they actually are,
but we see them, those objects, as we imagine them to be in our pro-
jections. Anyhow, in this down state and high state the physical
universe is two different things, two universes. As well as is the indi-
vidual universe.

The Peyote is a medicine. However it does it, it opens the individ-
ual or Human Universe again. Everything is pre-Greek looking out
into a universe of actual matter and spirits—actual spirits. (These
last not too clear sometimes, not even there at each moment, but
there. And some things more than spirits. An Osprey—I saw an
Osprey, a giant cartoon of an Osprey in the clouds, and I battled
him. Who is to say this isn't real?—It happened to me and I
wouldn't say it isn't real. Or maybe it was a hallucination—but
what is more real than a hallucination? And what would be more
animal, pre-Greek, or individual, than a hallucination? Or for that
matter what would be more possible than seeing something real
that is blotted out by a web? Or maybe it was real and anyone could
see it who had been there. My wife saw the Osprey—but not quite
in the same way. However, she did see me make the clouds disap-
pear and reappear at will.)

I was put in a primeval relationship to what I take to be reality
(reality as perfectly as I conceive it with my sense). Peyote is also
tainted or flavored with something that is Indian—so I had In-
dian-like thoughts. It was very strange in that sense. Perhaps it
was also that I realized the vastness of space and consequently
thought of plains sometimes as symbols of the space; though in
reality, Space, I saw, was simply vast beyond speaking of (only a
conception) and it is blue-gray and it is not the blackness of spaces
between stars. But perhaps these things come out of the Human
Universe. The kind of truths that Lawrence has in his *Apocalypse*

rather than material reality. And then again, these are truths because they are truths coming out of truths and perhaps an adjustment. (Perhaps this is rhetoric in its best sense.) For the first time in my life I knew that I was in absolute realistic perception of what occurred around me and within me. Also there is no need for thought in a peyote high. *Know thyself* is the most comical idea. Everything is known—to sense something with the senses is to know it. TO KNOW IT ABSOLUTELY. Without doubt or thought. Some synapse is avoided, it is so direct, there is no strange channeling of impulse to confusion or doubt to action.

That letter to Charles Olson begins to close the circling movement of these essays, as it amplifies the opening description of the peyote experience. The second section, "Wolf Net," begins another arc. But first I shall continue the thrust of my assertion that poetry is an organismic, complex act of a complex creature who is both matter and flesh in a universe that is matter, and flesh, and nothing less.

This idea has a history and development. To show its history in the process of thought will help. A year or so after writing the letter to Charles Olson describing the peyote state, I sent him a manifesto that I wrote to elucidate the thrust of my work to myself and to anyone who would care or listen. The egoism is that of a young man trying hard to see and feel clearly, and at the same time both sure and unsure of himself. I was in psychic pain or I might have made a more lucid statement, but the pain was in some senses a payment for the insights.

The manifesto was called "The Rose Flush, Straight Speech, Exclamation and the Drift."

In pure writing—by that I mean writing that is impure, writing that comes from the pre-anagogic desire centers—there is nothing to cling to in its shape save the morphological fact on the page. To clarify the beauty of Revolution I will name four elements found in my writings.

There is a claim made by philologists that thought follows speech, and action comes *through* speech or is a blockading or enactment of speech. This is perhaps true for a group of men. Certainly the Negative Capability of Keats is a way of action for some men and is to be seen as such. I am not sure about that philological conception, I believe that it may exist, but more I believe it is likely, if existent, as a mode, a domestication of the individual to a concept of his own relativity. Or perhaps a genetic incapability. I say it is a sickness. The use of writing is not to *lead out* but to enact and create appendages of the body, of personal physiology. Making a radiance or darkness into an actual morphological part, an extension even. But more a physiological part. An action and an action to be known by.

There is a tradition of exstasis, out of body, this is a religious tradition and is an accomplished fact. The work of a mantic. It may or may not have to do with Vision, Sight, it is concerned with being out of the body and is *accomplished* not anagogic.

I distinguish between an enacted tradition (mantic), and a concept (anagogic); the anagogic denies the objects of surroundings and intends to lead out to beauty that does not exist and is a confusion making an unwholesomeness. This is not the same as a courageous statement in a drama of Shakespeare or John Webster that calls us to perform a bold or proud action. Such statements come from the deep desire of a man for noble action, they do not lead out to unexistent beauty but to action. They are not anagogic, and likely never mantic. The existence of physiological writing is not to fill a form of false beauty.

My writing belongs to neither tradition but is a Revolution, sole and unrelated to the above. My writing deals with morphology (mine), physiology, and Sight and Senses. Not mimicry, but each writing a morphological existence independent except of myself. I do not duplicate the outside world but match my desires against it from my body. If I image, I do not present a virtual but an actual image. My writing is without scale and as unmeasurable as I am. Who is to tell me my size, or know it but myself? Dante, John Webster, Artaud, Lawrence, Boehme, are Western precursors of physiological writing.

A correspondent writes me: "Poetry isn't something to quote but something to live and die." Not lines written in perfection to be saved for the traditional beauty of their imagery and variance of traditional senses and imagery. A writing, if physiological, is an existent appendage of a total energy charge, not a compilation of formal variances but a direct (not virtual) manifestation of gene-deep feelings. Not anagogic!

In the morphology of my writing I find the *Drift,* the space, temporary cessation, nothing is there, I pass, leaving the blankness on the page and start when the drift is passed. I do not close the drifts, and I attempt an appoximation of their length, always momentary—but long to me as I drift.

Straight speech: (Pneumas, Connection of the flow of Kundalini through the chakras, Odem-speech, inspiration, not that these are the same things, I do not equate them.) The contact and straight carry-over of the feeling and creation of the physiology onto the page. As fine as blood or breathing, sureness, clarity dark or luminous direct. A lucid connection with my deep self whether in darkness or light. Rapid flow of truly spoken desires or feelings.

Exclamation: The sudden sight spoken, whether significant or not, not wisdom, the sudden sight. A seeing, Sensing, spoken loudly by the suddenness and meaning of it. Not to be carried from the context of the morphology as wisdom. Not quotable only speakable. A sight! Not usable, a sight!

The Rose Flush comes as a flower is supposed to. A flush comes to me as a hand is dealt in cards. A flush. An opening out to the softness of beauty or a *loveliness* of inspiration. The lines become longer less tensile there is a relaxation to a less deep (perhaps?) desire or reaction but to one of easier loved beauty. Opening like a spread hand of cards or a rose opening till it flattens before seeding. An ease at last perhaps after a straight speech that it is said, the morphos relaxes desires to give more, spreads its boundaries, its edge pushes out in exuberance. Language let in a little more. A pleasure or aid in the body of what's happening.   Dec. 10 '59

NOTE: The poem is a whole breath or group of breaths, the line (making shape) is a tensile manipulation, and should be felt as such. Esthetics is not a point! There is no prosody. The syllable is precisely a syllable and is to be read as a syllable, a heavy melody. The letter is exactly a letter.

In the statement I call attention to the pre-anagogic as a counterproposal to Olson's *anagogic*. For myself, in my own work I could not tolerate any idea that would lead me away from the *lapis philosophorum* of the alchemical gold. I was looking at the sensoriums of heroes. I was sensing through the eyes and nose of Shelley and John Webster, and using the hearing and touch of Ginsberg and Duncan and Kerouac—and the jazz lucidity of Creeley, and the Doug fir of Snyder, and the almost mystical, physical perceptions of D. H. Lawrence and of Olson himself. I was convinced that poetry was about, by, and from, the meat, that poetry was the product of flesh brushing itself against experience. We are seekers moving in the *Tathagata* brushing ourselves against the universe of real, solid illusions. It is by our touches that we become ourselves—as our ancestors became us and as we become our maturing, sharpening, brightening selves.

But enough of this talk of bodies—for one should not become obsessed with bodies unless one remembers the song that Su Tung-p'o sang a thousand years ago in the Sung Dynasty to the tune of the still older song "Immortal by the River."

Wai-Lim Yip translates the song character by character and then gives a versified translation of it. Character by character it reads:

1. night	drink	East	Slope	wake	again	drunk
2. return	—	it-seems	third	watch		
3. home	boy	nose-breath	already	thundering	—	
4. knock	door	all	no	response		
5. lean	staff	listen	river	sound		
6. long	regret	this	body	not	my	possession
7. when	—	forget	—	busy-buzz		
8. night	deep	wind	quiet	waves	—	smooth
9. small	boat	from	here	gone/drift		
10. river	sea	entrust	rest-of-life			

Professor Yip then versifies this way—it is not as good—but clearer:

Drinking into deep night at East Slope, sober then drunk.
I return home perhaps at small hours,
My page-boy's snoring already like thunder.
No answer to my knocking at the door,
I lean on my staff to listen to the river rushing.
I grieve forever that this body, no body of mine.
When can I forget this buzzing life?
Night now still, wind quiet, waves calm and smooth,
A little boat to drift from here.
On the river, on the sea, my remaining years.

Compare this much more recent poem by the Japanese hai-kuist Bashō—who came into life about the time Shakespeare expired in England:

Beneath the roof,
Drops of Spring rain
Trail slowly
Down the honeycomb.

The haunting quality of such poems shakes the planking of our very real existence, as does the manfully solid despair of Olson's alternating grief and exuberance in *Maximus Volume Three*. The final volume of his epic calls the shadow play of the world into clear sight:

the left hand is the calyx of the Flower
can cup all things within itself, nothing else
there, itself, alone limb of being, acting
in the beneficent air, holding all tenderness
as though it were the soul itself, the Soul's
limb

For years I have been intrigued by a poem because of the grace of its diction, the beauty of the statement it makes, and

its elegance—the elegance that one finds in Bud Powell play-
ing "Autumn in New York" or in the compositions of Thelo-
nius Monk. The poem is by Otomo Yakamochi. It is from
eighth-century Japan and is included in the *Manyōshū* an-
thology. The poem was sent with orange blossoms to Lady
Otomo of Sakanoe's elder daughter:

While I waited and wondered,
  The orange-tree that grows in my garden,
Spreading out a hundred branches,
Has burst into bloom, as the fifth month
For garland-making draws near.
Every morning and every day I go out
To see the flowers and keep close guard,
Lest they should fall off
Before you, whom I love as the breath of life,
Have seen them once on a night when the moon
Is clear as a shining mirror.
But the wicked cuckoo,
Though I chase him again and again,
Comes crying in the sad hours of dawn
And wantonly scatters the blooms on the ground.
Knowing not what to do,
I have reached and broken off these with my hand,
Pray, see them, my lady!

Envoys

These are the orange-blossoms of my garden
I had intended you to see
Some time after mid-month
On a clear moonlight night.

The cuckoo has scattered
My orange-blooms on the ground.
Oh, had he only come
After you had seen the flowers!

It is the elegance of the loop systems of this poem—almost like visceral and muscular feedback or the play of the nervous system—that makes me feel it is close to being a living thing.

THE SURGE
for Brakhage

This is the failure of an attempt to write a beautiful poem. I would like to have it looked at as the mindless coiling of a protein that has not fully achieved life—but one that is, or might be, a step towards living-being.

THE SURGE! THE SURGE! THE SURGE!
IT IS THE SURGE OF LIFE
I SEEK
TO VIEW . . .

Plato and Darwin are the dead heads of glorious vision.

Dante turned to the woman Beatrice
in Paradiso and she spoke:
"Tis true that oftentimes the shape
will fail to harmonize with the design
when the material is deaf to answer.
Then from its course the creature deviates;
For though impelled towards the highest heaven
it has the power to bend in other ways—
just as when fire is seen to fall from clouds
if the first impulse of its natural bent,
turned by false pleasure, drives it to the earth.
—No more, if I judge rightly,
shouldst thou marvel
at thy ascent, than at a falling rill
that plunges from the mountain to the depths.
T'would be as strange, hadst thou stayed down below . . ."

IS NOT THE OLD MALE BEAST SIGHT OF IT
as dead as Hell?
Our view of Life is still so young and so worn
and ripped by the brutal tatters we made of it!
Subtle Plato and Darwin opened worlds to us by stating
what we knew and our admissions threw us into
reality! How blind is blind?
How deaf and dumb is our dumbness? If we admit,
we do have fresher eyes. There's a calm inertness
of joy that living beings drift to and from. (And it is far
back when the Universe began . . .
and it is here now too.) I do not mean the mystic's view.
Or that of a man locked in the superstition of his own repression.
Not emotive analogies!
I mean there is a more total view!
It shifts and changes and wavers,
and weakens as our nerves do, to finally make
a greater field and more total sight.
We yearn for it . . .

I love you is the key.

The Surge of Life may not be seen by male or female
for both are halves. But perhaps the female,
who is unprincipled, sees farther and into more.

2.

OH, HOW I HAVE BEAT MY HEAD AT IT in male stupidity!
And here . . . here in my hand, is a picture of the living Universe
made by a woman as gift of love in a casual moment!
—A valentine in ballpoint ink. The drawing calls all
previous images to abeyance. The dark and radiant
swirlings in my head seem clumsy—tho I trust them too.
It is a tree that is not a tree.
It might be a placenta with thin branches or veins.
The stalk of it narrows to a gasp of life
and stretches downward and spreads into what

might be the earth or the top of another tree.
((Is there a forest?))
(Upon the lower treetop, or earth, lies a creature coiled
and incomplete, with round and staring eyes.)
Intersecting the narrow trunk, or crossing it, in
mysterious geometry, is a palette shape.
Upon it spins around and round, before ascending
up the stalk into the boughs, a creature that
is a ring of meat divided into the individuals
comprising it. They are hot upon each other's
tails. They stare after one another and outwards
with round eyes. Some beasts of the ring
are dots and blobs or teardrops of primal meat.
And some are more whole creatures. Some contain
within themselves, midway, an extra pair of eyes
to show their division is not complete. (Or
to assert the meaninglessness of all division
that is based on eyes or other organs.) Those eyes
deny that a single head or set of senses divide
lifes in a greater sense. *The ring is one!*
The creatures
swell, spring free, and dart up the cincture
to a greater space above.

A long, large, snake-shaped molecule of flesh
coils from the earth
around the palette and caresses the higher branch
in sensuality.
The high part is a heart! Within it a man's head & shoulders
rise from a bat-winged heart with thready tail—
and a heart upon the thread tip. Nearby is a circle
(a vacuole? a nucleus?) with a shape inside that might
be any living thing from a vulture to a child.

High and low outside are stars that are
living sparks or moths.
Turned upside down the drawing means
not more nor less. It is a gentle
tensile surge
a woman views.

3.

Yes, all things flow! And in our male insistency on meaning
we miss the truth. The mountains do pour, moving in millionic
ripples over thousand aeons. Demanding brute reality we forget
the greater flow and then the black immediate is larger—and it is
and isn't. But Life, THE PLASM, does not flow like lead does.
It SURGES! Is that the difference?—And it is one great whole
and isn't. It is something sweeter than we see—we must feel
and hear it too! Male and female have, and do not have, importance.
They matter! *It is not relative but real!*
In black immediate I feel the roaring meat mountain
herds of Bison and of Whales or Men or solid
American clouds of birds 100 years ago.
Then I am moved by meanings and sights of
the smaller surge! Then I, dreaming,
partake in the surge like a Plains Indian
on horseback and I know my smallest gene
particles are forever spread and immortal. Distances
and hallucinations then can cause no fear;
life is primitive and acceptable.

Is all life a vast chromosome stretched in Time?
Simply a pattern for another thing?
But the pattern like the chromosomes *is* the Life,
and the Surge is its vehicle.

It does not matter!

It is the athletic living thing of energy!
All else is *soundless and sightless* pouring.

There is no teleology but
surging freedom.

Inert matters pour in and out of the Surge
and make sound and sight. But neither
they nor the Surge will wait. It is another matter.

Space/Space/Space is a black lily holding the rosy,
full, flowing, and everspreading and con-
tracting, spilling flash.

The woman's easy sight of it can be bolder than the man's
She admits that we can never know, and tells
us that the question is useless words.
The Surge can never see itself for the Surge is
its self-sight. And its sight
and being are simultaneous.
There is no urge to see or feel—for it *is* sight
and feeling.

Except for the glory

GLORY

GLORY

GLORY

GLORY

GLORY

GLORY

it does not matter.

4.

But desire to know and feel are not eased!
To feel the caves of body and the separate
physical tug of each desire is insanity. The key
is love
and yearning. The cold sea beasts

and mindless creatures are the holders of vastest
Philosophy.
We can never touch it.
We are blessed.

Praise to the Surge of life that there is no answer
—and no question!

Genetics and memory

are the same

they are degrees of one

molecular unity.

We are bulks of revolt and systems of love-structuring
in a greater whole
beginning where the atoms come
to move together and make a coiling string . . .

Beyond the barrier
all things are laid upon a solid
and at rest.

Beatrice! Beatrice! *Paradiso is opening.*

WE ARE AT THE GATES OF THE CHERUBIC!

Part Two

WOLF NET

For Sterling Bunnell

I.
MOZART AND THE APPLE

WHEN A MAN DOES NOT ADMIT THAT HE IS AN ANI-MAL, he is less than an animal. Not more but less.

I have heard that Mozart signed letters to his sister with endearing obscenities such as, "a kiss on the bottom to my darling sister." Watch young animals at play, the endearments, the mutual explorations and cleanings, the investigations. In the human realm these cub activities are forbidden or left in the secrecy of dark closets, basements, and silent bedrooms.

Mozart might be merry, tortured, brooding, serious, all at once. An animal lives in many states. The man who cannot see that he is an animal is trapped in a maze with a beginning and an end. The beginning is obviously birth and the end is apparently death.

*

Cyril Connolly states that memory is a sieve and that large and important data pieces will not pass through the weave.

An animal does not specialize in a discipline. He puts the large chunks that will not pass through the sieve into an aggregate to ensure his survival. The wolf is not a wandering scholar but a wandering minstrel—with the whole prairie for an auditorium and world-field to work upon. He can visualize a universe of sound as a field on which to conceive and topologize his personal statements. Mozart might be seen as a kind of wolf at play. His merry greeting to his sister's bottom might be

a wolfish act of comic grace coming from a higher state of psychic freedom, rather than from the maze a domesticated creature is trained to run in.

*

Pieces of information can come together in hieroglyphs and conformations that are beyond our normal enmazed remembrances and experiences. CHILDHOOD IS AN OVERWHELMING VISION IN REMEMBERING. CERTAINLY IT IS AN OVERWHELMING EXPERIENCE. The remembrance of the absurdities, pains, joys, INTENSITIES, preposterousnesses, agonies, sensualities, freedoms, cages, punishments, and rewards staggers the comprehension! In remembrance childhood illuminates the rememberer or recasts the old nets of familiarity and rebuilds the forgotten bridges and barriers of hates, loves, and predispositions.

To remember the chairs of childhood is to reevaluate the chairs of now.

*

The artist considers himself a realist trapped in a vision. He knows that with the twenty-seven senses he is given, and without an infinite number of senses, he can make constructs of only the most fractional semblances of the total matter he swirls in (or that thrashes or dreams in him).

The pieces of his experience and remembrance and perception, writing themselves upon his sensorium, come together in strange modalities and proportions and combinations. He believes he perceives REALISTICALLY more than it is possible to have seen. (He must lose the fear of being wrong.) As a realist he trained himself for perception-as-vision, or he was born with the capacity and chose to develop it.

Surely the most Augustan artists cherished secret acknowledgements of their Romance—perhaps Horace frightened himself as his view of structure expanded and contracted. Seneca was privy to a court that made his blood-revenge dramas seem as frothy as the plays of Noel Coward.

Seneca's death was a grotesque, noble absurdity. He escaped from the mafia-esque court of Nero (after being an apologist for monsterhood), then was condemned to death by the Emperor. The sentry tapped his foot outside Seneca's door, while one suicide attempt after another failed, until finally, with bleeding wrists, weeping wife, numbed by slow-working hemlock, dictating his death hexameters, he was carried by his slaves into a vapor bath, where he kissed final good-bye to his *geist* amidst the steam.

*

We are the most complex formations of physical matter on this planet surface. We are born out of physical matter from a spectrum of inorganic matter that shapes itself into amino acids, bacteria, viruses, sponges, and ultimately projects the vertebrate. The vertebrate creature coexists with life forms just as perfect, merely less complex.

It is the nature of certain matter, under special conditions, to become a growing surge producing more and more physically complex and subjectively intense types. In the 1920s and 1930s it was accepted that there is no teleological outcome to this process. Sensations of hopelessness, nausea, horror, were the result. The discoveries demanded a new bourgeois ethic for the intellectual and professional man.

But the development of the Existentialist ethic was interrupted by World War Two (a manifestation of nationalistic evangelisms and the endocrine stress of overpopulation). Camus and Sartre confronted the raw prehensions of the biological frontier sciences—and the apparent meaninglessness of life. However, their solution met, head-on, the sealing-up of a planetary industrial society at war with itself.

*

If experience-information (memory) is stored hologramistical-
ly within the brain, that is, if the memory constructs are stored
throughout the brain, and not in units in certain areas, it
would do much to explain imagination and creative thought.
This implies that storage is not stationary. As one constellation
of memories lights up, and becomes an awareness, it illumi-
nates partially, and possibly *in toto,* the adjacent, intercon-
nected, or associated nets and constellations of information.
The activity is constant, or is an off/on process. Or, it might be
multiple, constant, interrelating processes.

Played against the constant shows of stored experience pat-
terns is the intake of new immediate experience through the
apertures of the sensorium—the eyes, ears, nose, etc.

*

While I am stimulated by the novelty of an immediate experi-
ence it continues to register as the primary experience. I hold
an apple in my hand. I am entertained by the odor, the color,
the reflections of light, the irregularities of the natural shape. I
experience the weight, the density, the temperature of the ap-
ple. I am not hungry, the apple is an esthetic object.

Assume that I have a three-dimensional screen within my
head (perhaps it is the reticular formation). What I feel, see,
think, and know is imaged on the screen. This screen IS the
best image that I can make, with limited senses, of the world
and universe surrounding me. It is also the neuron-sculptural
screen for memory-experience activity that continuously dances.
There appears to be an order of preference for what takes
place on the sculpture screen. The order is apparently biological.

*

While the apple is interesting it continues to register. As I ex-
plore it, it grows less interesting. It becomes a familiar object.
It recedes into the "category" *apple.* However, it becomes
APPLE again as I study it more and sensory interest revives. At

last it becomes category again. But it becomes category gradually and by default. It becomes stored information, if it stimulates me to remember or speak of it, if I make it a piece that will not pass through the sieve.

While this APPLE is the center of my attention, while it occupies the primary area of the screen, there are associations of stored information playing at the screen's edges. I compare this apple to another apple—its similarities and dissimilarities. The APPLE *may* become hologramistically stored as a memory and it may interrelate with other apples, or with other memories connected with apples. (((The *odor* of the apple may stimulate nonverbal, nonintellective, nonrational parts of my consciousness that send apple-related associations to the periphery of the screen. The *touch* of the apple might do the same. The noise of a truck sloshing on the street through the rain might bring childhood images to the edges of the screen that is concerned with APPLE. Childhood rain images may light up childhood apple images, or illuminate a fleeting picture of youth that contains both apple and rain—such as eating an apple on a rainy trick-or-treat jaunt.)))

APPLE is the center of my attention, of the three-dimensional screen. At its edge flicker images that are there by chance and by associations of odor, touch, or hearing.

*

It is the nature of animal life to keep moving. The cytoplasm flows and ripples in the cell. Every life is part of the total surge of Life that feeds upon itself as it expands in size and complexity. The whole surge is powered by the sun. It becomes more complex. It grows. It expands. It is a retopologizing of the surface of the planet brought about by direct energy. Animal life keeps moving. It moves to eat, or it moves to keep from being eaten. —Or both.

The human mammal body, in the billions of years of the evolution of its complexity, has concretized the necessity to keep moving. The retopologizing surge (changing inert matter into organic) does not slow down. It will not stop exchanging parts of itself as nourishment in the expansion of the energized complexity. Oxygen, nitrogen, carbon, hydrogen, sulfur, combined with the sun's energy, become pandas, salmon, roses, blackberries. Creatures move!

*

The desire for movement is internalized. In my case the desire is to write a poem. As the apple recedes, the longing to write a poem begins to produce a new image—the image of a poem, the sound of a poem—the image of a bison. The desire to write a poem about bison takes over the periphery of the image screen, perhaps the poem-desire incorporates apple-related images—or rejects them.

I am sitting with an apple in my hand but no apple on the screen. On the sculptural screen is the image of a herd of bison driven by thirst, crashing into the mudflats of a summer river on the plains. They are followed by a pack of wolves laughing like Mozarts.

II.
PIECES OF BEING

A: TOUCHING THE MIME

As if enacting a mimesis, men, after their destruction of the giant mammals, have taken over within their own species the ecological roles of predator and prey. They act out the fundamental fact that life is an expanding river that feeds and beats upon itself. (It is the nature of life to move, to explore, to acquire territories, and to preserve the acquisitions for descendants.) The body of perceptions and intellect that arises in flashes during the turmoil becomes frozen as books, electronics, statutes, doctrines, philosophies, arts, oral traditions, cathedrals, religions. They become solidified in patterns and structures that serve the general and continuing holocaust.

As population increases, sensitivity of creature to creature becomes more profound, intense, and brutalized.

*

For artist or animal there is but one religion. At first glance it is simple. As simple as the animal (a sessile polyp or sea cucumber) or as complex as the animal's nervous system — as with a dolphin, a panda, or a man. The religion is *being* itself.

Being is the creature's contact with its surroundings and the accumulation of instinct and experience-information. An animal's contact with its environment is obviously physical. Storage and circulation of information is material (atomic, molecular, chemical).

In the religion of *being* the universe is the Messiah. For the creature to know itself it must touch physically, or reconstellate information. Without touch, sight, taste, smell, affective perception, memory, and imagination there can be no body image. If there is no body there is no being. All life is sensate and sensitive. Life is aware of itself by the abrasion of the so-called inorganic world, or by the touch of creatures in the organic world.

*

We have a given number of senses to perceive the outward universe—and yet we can easily imagine, or intuit, that the universe is infinite both dimensionally and as a field for undreamed senses.

A ribosome in a liver cell in a salmon might relate to a field of energies or a point within a quasar or a distant sun. There might be interlocked and predisposed relationships of these and other constructs. If the universe is a single flow or aura, it seems highly likely that such interrelationships exist. (And the universe IS indeed an aura of trillionically multiplex interrelations. And it is primarily comprised of styles of matter that we do not consciously contact.) We cannot perceive an antimatter universe—yet everything that we perceive as real might be an empty pinprick of nothingness within a nirvana of antimatter beyond comprehension.

*

All life is a single unitary surge, a giant organism—even a single spectacular protein molecule. It is not possible to imagine (in view of its whirlwind energy and delicate complexity) that in the four billion years life has grown on this planet there have not developed interacting fields and forces within its behemoth topology. If life could be seen as a structure, not against a background of time, but all at once as a freestanding sculpture, the sight would be illuminating and staggering. We would then form new concepts of interrelations of life.

As a creature presses itself against its physical environment, known and unknown, conscious and unconscious, it discovers the contours of its body. In growth, death, injury, expansion, contraction, movement, perception, it discovers and forms itself from the genetic possibilities that it contains. It fills a pattern and becomes an individual in the precise and unique blowup of the generalized possible construct.

*

The universe is the Messiah because it is the possibility of our being. We are that Messiah, yet we brush, hurl, and gently touch our beings against it to experience it. Our experience of the universe is also the universe perceiving itself. One point of perception is no less subjectively relevant than another—all are part of a whole. Subjectivity and objectivity resolve themselves as meaningless scratches on a graph.

*

We CAN imagine ourselves to be the universe experiencing itself—and the universe as the field and background for our self-experience. If we realize that the relative importance of occurrence to occurrence is a judgement and not insight into Nature—then we are free to feel biologically that each point of perception is of importance.

Each life is a tentacle or finger of the Messiah or Tathagata experiencing self and the universe through entrances of perception, movement, and contact. But to assign the Messiah human nature any more than the nature of a sea cucumber is beyond reason.

We are not more alive than an amoeba—we are more complex. We are multiple trillions of cells, a miniature universe of molecules, rather than stars. As we are clusters of cells in a multiplex structure, we are also not a SELF or an INTELLI-GENCE. We are congresses of SELVES and of INTELLI-GENCES. When the congress agrees we please ourselves.

*

Cro-Magnon man was a superior man-animal in obvious bio-logical respects. His brain size was larger than contemporary man's—about the size of the dolphin's. If Cro-Magnon man was less subject to degenerative diseases and less prone to modern genetic and actual defects such as caries and tuberculosis, the artist could idealize him and begin a review of history from that point.

Relics of sympathetic hunting magic still stand—earth altars, clay mounds over which an animal skin was stretched. (The earliest altars were representations of animals. Only later did man place his image there so that he might see himself *ex-alter*.) Is it right to view this rite of hunting magic as approximating religion? There are inherent animal rituals: a father makes faces at his child; children hide and jump out at each other; a man sneaks up on his wife and kisses her—as a wolf does with his bitch. These are natural animal games and rites. They fulfill a shape of training, or act out internalized desires and energies. The actions express instinctive longings, are re-arrangements of perceptions and activities that stimulate a ludic sense. It is speculation that the Paleolithic altars, punctured with spear holes, and the wall paintings, are sympathetic magic. It is as likely that they were a game performed in moments of leisure—or to recall pleasures of the hunt.

It is as likely that Cro-Magnon WAS a religious being, did conceive of himself and the universe as a reality, a dream, a structure he partook of. Keats and a wolf have no need for institutionalized religion. They seem fully pleased to perceive external and personal being. Agnostic Keats said that life is the Vale of Soul-making.

The mystic Meister Eckhart held that belief in God might debilitate the religious experience. To presume to "know" God's shape, form, color, size, and temperament narrows perceptions. The expectation inhibits clear sight by making rigid structures upon which experience must be hung, or a graph against which all things must be seen.

B: THE OPENING SYSTEM (AN INTERLUDE)

Traditional science of the early twentieth century, before the frontier science of microbiology developed in the 1950s, saw the animal cell as a container—a closed system open to chemical transfers. The cell was seen as an enclosed unit capable of reproducing itself. Now the cell is seen as a complex system that is the center of life, with complements of symbiotic mini-organs and highly complicated life constructs on atomic and molecular levels.

The new scientific vision sees life creating itself *outward* from the minutest physical level to the macroscopic world of muscles, organs, perceptions of the senses, and animal activities. Till now man has looked into himself to see technically how HE *works*. The process is in reversal. We look to the sub-microscopic to discover how we are *created*—how the molecules become structures in a cell, how they coil themselves and move strings of acids carrying messages and directions, how the cells make the types of meat. At last, finally, the CREA-TURE is visible. This is an absolute shift in vision that alters our relationship to the bodies, atoms, and subatomic particles in our finger as well as to those in outer and distant space.

C: NEOLITHIC AESTHETICS

One theory of aesthetics contends that Neolithic art is the product of stress—of cultural anxiety and longing. The traceries and intertwined geometrical patterns on a shield are seen to be faces staring out with wide eyes of fear, rage, and anger. The art of the Neolithic resembles nothing so much as the front and rear views of automobiles. The bulging eyes of the headlights and grimace of bumpers contends with the frown or astonished gasp of the grill.

No human creature is able to be in normal waking state in the presence of another without an acknowledgement of the other's creature-presence. Each has an invisible bubble of personal, private, territorial space about himself. One can violate this by choice, drawing close to another or to others. Then the bubbles merge, go down, and can even conjoin. The bubble can burst when the man is overwrought by the continual nearness of others—and the unflagging necessity to cope with internalized reactions to others. Presumably the bubble can mutate and become a bubble of another shape and manner through accustomization. (Look at the ritelike manners of traditional Japan.)

When the bubble is continuously violated, man loses his sense of individuality, the uniqueness of his personal perceptions. When he too often experiences, directly or indirectly, the sensations of too many others, the bubbles of all involved in the collusion burst and the individuality of all is weakened. Then man is not so much a social animal as a mass animal—a being living with compromised perceptions. The individual's geniuses and talents and intelligences become useless in the mass situation.

*

The "primitive" artist in a crowded Neolithic situation feels himself in a maze. With a knife, or paint, or tattooing needle, he makes an image of the lines of stress that his personal uniqueness confronts in the distortions and repressions of his group. All artists make self-portraits. He makes a portrait from the geometry and it reflects his own hidden features of fear or rage.

The more violent of a population extend their geometrical perceptions upon a world no longer clear to them. The curved linear projection of rage, puzzlement, and fear is used to adorn a war shield, then the outer universe is attacked. Man begins to conceive himself as a tool of himself—and of others. He moves into the confusion encircling him. He attacks the soil. He attacks the trees, he attacks other men. He begins to use blood sacrifice (animals then men then war) as a means of heightening through intensity the hope of obliterating the new geometry of confusion.

((Earlier, Cro-Magnon man must have recognized the independent creature-being of the large animals that he killed and ate. He saw them as living equals, companions in the stream of life that surged about him. To kill the creature was good. It was not good to be killed by another creature. He had an elementary mammal code. He could see that his cousin creatures partook of the same code and were equally alive. He was at the top of a system involving his cousin creatures. He did not see this placement as superior or inferior but perhaps as luck—or as a battle he had won with strong opponents. He might have been conscious of his genetic inheritance.))

*

Neolithic men raised their cousin creatures about them. The ungulates, dogs, swine, and sheep, grew up close to the family. The young man, or woman, or babe could see the creature being slaughtered. They must have been aware of cousinship to these creatures and moved by the sacrifice. They knew that these animals were prisoners kept for food sacrifice or labor.

Man had been an independent being, and had evolved as a

free creature. The presence of domesticated animals must have moved against some high-spirited creature-sense and caused grief.

The domestication of animals concomitant with the cultivation of plants allowed the population surge in the post-Neolithic period. The abundance of food and the need for workers acted together to create a cultural system.

As population surges, the members of populations become literally addicted to the presence of numbers of their kind. This has been clearly shown in studies of overpopulation in animal colonies. As the spiral forms, population addiction increases population—then density of population increases the addiction. At the opening of the Neolithic population swell there was more cultivation and more expansion of domesticated animal species to support the growth. Among men there began a new breeding. It was a breeding away from individuality and towards a laboring, docile, group-submissive type. (In

an age so obsessed with drugs and addiction to drugs, observations on the root addiction to population might shed light on the fears of, and expansion of, narcotics addiction—especially at a time when there is so much need for reconstruction, and so little time for narcosis. Drugs might be the extension of an inherent tendency to addictions, more a symptom than a problem in themselves.)

As some members of the group felt anguish for domestic creatures slaughtered to keep population growing, the stress of the group increased. Simultaneously the domesticated and

cultivated foodstuffs became more effete genetically and bio-
chemically in trace elements and natural glandular and hor-
monic compounds. The land around the settlement was de-
pleted and livestock was in the process of controlled genetic
alteration. The Neolithic consumer began to chemically alter
himself. Plants will grow in less than optimum chemical cir-
cumstances and less than optimum plants result. Less than op-
timum men combined in an unintentional selective breeding
for a directable, socially docile, less individualistic

        NEW

            type

          of

            MAN (beginning

    to oppose himself to MAMMAL.)

III.
BLAKE AND THE YOGIN

WHEN A MAN DOES NOT ADMIT HE IS AN ANIMAL, he is less than an animal. The great MAMMAL William Blake is of importance for the beauty he presents, for the clarity of his vision, and for his example. The reader may give himself to Blake to experience an invention. The invention might be called a "systemless system." It goes against societal precepts by being outside of society. It is based on clarity of his perceptions and his rejection of the general propaganda. Blake's intuitive meditative imagination employed his unique reconstellation of sensory data, creating new models.

The structure of Blake is so durable that it is an actual artifact. It remains an island of clarity in a culture that would have rejected Blake as a madman or useless visionary repellent to the self-domesticated society.

Blake is as present today as if he were biologically alive. His works are extensions of himself. ((A contemporary example is the *spiritual moment* of Abstract Expressionism in which the painter created transcriptions of arm and brush that are statements, like pawprints of physical being. Wolfprints!))

Blake's works, like the artifacts of all high artists, are his body. Gestures come so directly from his physical being that their presence is real and physical. Blake appeared to Allen Ginsberg in a vision. In adolescence I dreamed I was Blake. Blake seemed as real a presence as an automobile.

*

Blake withdrew as fully and wholly as he could and still persevere in his daily labors. He contributed minimally to society, defied it often, refused to be put into a niche by it. Blake was as private as his reason allowed. He took what he could use, as a hunter, and rejected—or struggled against—what was offensive to him. Blake was the revolt of one man. He was not a revolutionary but a man in revolt. A creature in *revolt* can conceive that there is NO solution and that there will be unending construction and destruction. REVOLT perceives the continuance of action and energy from multiple sources.

Revolt perceives that life is a flow and must be constantly dealt with—and that there must be constant experience. To cease experience, or to imagine utopian bliss, is like the imaginings of nirvana—interesting, but not for long, and unless challenging—ultimately dulling and stupefying.

A creature must be maintained internally or there can be no revolt (*revolution* looks to the *outside* for answers). Blake revolted with his being and maintained himself as a visionary mammal as best he might in his circumstances. His creature pride and his vision in works of poetry and painting survive as part of his body. REVOLT IS A BIOLOGICAL PROCESS.

*

MAN IS NOT AN ISOMER OF MAMMAL—he is precisely mammal. The route to this awareness is necessarily biological. *Poetry is biological.*

In his childhood Blake wrote one of the perfect lyrics:

How sweet I roam'd from field to field,
    And tasted all the summer's pride,
Till I the prince of love beheld,
    Who in the sunny beams did glide!

He shew'd me lilies for my hair,
  And blushing roses for my brow;
He led me through his gardens fair,
  Where all his golden pleasures grow.

With sweet May dews my wings were wet,
  And Phoebus fir'd my vocal rage;
He caught me in his silken net,
  And shut me in his golden cage.

He loves to sit and hear me sing,
  Then, laughing, sports and plays with me;
Then stretches out my golden wing,
  And mocks my loss of liberty.

   This song, the early prophetic work *The Marriage of Heaven and Hell,* and the *Songs of Innocence and Experience* tell us, now, what the end of the last century and the opening of this one labored to produce in mythologies of psychology. (Ego, Id, Oedipalism, Anima, replace the fairy folk of the country in the confines of the city. Trolls, brownies, leprechauns, pookas doff their country costumes for the abstractions of new folklore.)

*

The yogin seeks awareness of the universe through meditation. He fixes upon an object or pattern till his intellective processes are emptied. *Then* the true vision, *mukti,* will perform itself upon the processes of the sensorium. This is done through infinite attention to study, regimen, concentration, or combinations of these and other techniques.

   The Indonesian mystic Pak Subu made a discovery. His discovery, when freed of the trappings of prayer and evangelism, is that in giving apparently free rein to the muscular and organic movements of the body, the body becomes filled with sensation of itself and achieves a transcendental state. During the Subud ceremony one spontaneously exercises from the muscles and organs, and as unconsciously as possible. The organs sing rhythmically, and are freed of the censorship of the mind by the social reinforcement of others who participate likewise. Beyond doubt the stress of culture in the area of Indonesian population density gave birth to this cult as much as did a vision. —The need to be free.

*

There are at least three ways of emptying the sensory system. One is the practice of yoga or meditation—to willfully, studiously, methodically train the body-mind to focus on blankness. Another way to reach this state was *Boga*. Members of society who could not practice Yoga, or who because of class or obligation were unable to follow the first path, sometimes chose the second path. Boga was a celebration of the emptiness of the senses that was achieved by surfeit of the senses. Those following the path of Boga met and filled themselves with meat (forbidden), parched grain (forbidden), wine (forbidden) and sexuality. Trying to find nirvanic bliss, one caught, through overfullness, a view beyond the world veil of Maya. The senses were whited out by fulfillment. Boga was performed as a religious act.

A third method of clearing the senses can be seen in Pak Subu's Subud cult, and in dervishism and perhaps Hassidic dancing.

An experiment: In privacy allow the muscles of the body to do anything they please, to twist and turn as a baby does on a rug in the sunlight. The eyes are closed and the vocal apparatus begins to respond to the pleasure of the societally negated postures of the body (as one groans automatically under the hands of a masseur). The eyes are closed or squinted, and there is little or no visual stimulation. At first it is difficult to purposelessly writhe, twist, groan, cry, sing, chant, kick, twist, moan, weep, or laugh. Eventually, and after practice, after a number of trials, a mindless biological state is found. It then becomes easier to find the state and one may exercise there longer and longer. If one develops this capacity up to thirty minutes or an hour, he finds on reclaiming his social person that he is in a euphoric state—a high. The senses see the brightness and auras and colors of objects about them and there is a feeling of physiological well-being. The experimenter will have been in a place where he, or she, was flying no banners but was a mammal—the universe experiencing itself.

*

The biological event goes back to the neuron screen upon which senses register. The screen has been so filled with spontaneous and automatic cries, conjoined with the unpremeditatable body movements, that there is no spot for the registration of associations, anxieties, longings, aspirations, hopes, daydreams, or anything but the body itself AS THE UNIVERSE. It is a move through the veil—perhaps not through the veil of Maya but certainly that of the milieu. A simpler experiment is to go to the top of a hill in a lonely place and shout, scream, or laugh for a few minutes. It will quickly be seen that it is impossible to scream and think at the same time. To feel the body as the universe of life and the universe of matter simultaneously is transcendental. Emptying the mind is clearing it through feedback. It is restful and sane.

*

The Greeks, recognizing the polytheistic nature of the traditional senses (that each was a god or goddess), had a motto. *Ariston metron* means, roughly, "moderation is highest." In the works of the Greek intellectives, we find they treasured drunkenness, songs, libations to the gods, the game of spitting wine into a bucket, meditation, commerce, warfare, athletics, travel, brilliance of conversation, extremes of sensuality. The Greek *intellective* (as contrasted to the more mental *intellec-*

tual) conceived of moderation as a personal structure, arrived at by the discovery and assertion of extremes. When a man went to extremes he found the outridings of possibilities and he WAS MODERATION—he was formed within the field of his experience.

The Chou Dynasty in China was a period of extremes, with ancestor and tiger and owl cults, divination, drunkenness and drinking songs, the need for strong tribalisms, mercantile and territorial wars, silks, sensualities, blood rites, love songs—a vigorous society. Insights into it may be found in the *I Ching, The Book of Songs,* the ethics of Confucius, and in the works of the Taoist thinkers. The successful man created his moderation—and yet cherished the notion of moderation. True moderation seems to be a projection of the interior creature.

*

Aristophanes opened his play *Peace* with slaves rolling balls of shit and tossing them over a barricade to a giant dung beetle. He presented lord and servant shitting in their pants, and showed dainty, grasping, gluttonous representations of the gods (that seem healthful in their audacity). His theatre was not psychological. Modern psychological realism is limited by its moderate possibilities. (Strindberg's work is the beautiful revolution of an intense, brilliant man—socially tortured by the extremes of his daily life—a man who was mad by "social" analysis.)

*

In the Tate Gallery in London hangs Blake's watercolor of Beatrice addressing Dante from the chariot. The chariot wheels are made of swirling creatures. Above the chariot are the alchemized signs of the four gospels: Mark, Matthew, Luke, and John. The chariot is drawn by monumental griffons. It is Dante's scene, and Blake's constellative perception frames itself against a scene from *Purgatorio.* Blake's imagination is nearly free. He allows the imagination to be as complex, and as colored, and as firmly lined as it will become in its own terms. HE LETS IT EXPAND until it forms a system for the illustration. He does not direct himself into a system, he lets one expand. One image after another continues until it structures a system. It is a system that is never fixed. It keeps moving, the watercolor invents its own rules—it extends Dante's vision. It becomes both illustration of Dante and a unique work that fits into Blake's expansively gyring being.

The *Divine Comedy* might be seen similarly. The *Inferno* is fascinating for its scenes of sensual horror, pathos, sympathy, all conjoined in intellective adventure. *Purgatorio* is more satisfying—the sensorium of *Inferno* has begun to constellate more imaginative and more real creatures and beings. Differences within *Purgatorio*'s monodic landscape are given more complexity. The stairs become living movies (as well might the stairways of our future, for the walls that surround us are mutilated with horrors of mercantilism). In *Paradiso* the eco-complexity becomes so intense with throngs and multitudes of the Divine that it flares into the feedback of an ultimate vision.

> Milton's Satan in Hell is reminiscent of NOW. Crowded, fallen angel to fallen angel. Would a sensitive man of Periclean Greece taken up from time and placed in the N.Y.C. Garment Center at rush hour, or in Peking, or Tokyo, or London, imagine himself in Hell? Or might he fall dead of stress impact as some deer do at the sound of a rifle shot?

*

It seems that Meat is thought. Meat is intellective. Brain cells, nerve cells—like any cells—are meat. They mime the functions of all other meat that expands while there is an energy source—forming a great being that beats and feeds upon itself. As an animal, man unconsciously mimes the process of being. Yet he gives service to a structure more and more cruel, not realizing the multitude of options open to any life or lives. He closes the box about him and topologizes complexities of maze upon maze within its confines.

*

THE BODY IS A FAIRYLAND—or, more correctly, is made up of congeries of FAIRYLANDS and ELFLANDS. The invention of the electron microscope has made it possible to view the micro-detail of cellular infrastructure, and X-ray diffraction techniques have enabled us to view the molecular structure of the cell. With mild enlargement (sixty magnifications) of the surface of the tongue, the tastebuds can be seen as a garden of beings serving to taste and to guide the macro-being. A skin pore magnified several thousand times is seen as a naturally irregular meat cave inhabited by bacteria.

Under electron magnification the sleek surface of the teeth is a multiplicity of fairy caverns. The structure of bone is an airy pixie lattice resembling the most fantastic constructions of calcareous sea creatures. The surface of the hand resembles an arid deltic plain. The hair is a forest. Under further magnification the surface of the hair is scaled and overlapped protein bark. The saucer-shaped red cells are entities—trillions of them move carrying oxygen and returning with CO_2. The phagocytes can be seen as shapefully shape-changing creatures extruding themselves to ingest harmful bacteria. Under intense magnification of the electron instrument the coiled genes of bacteria are visible. We can see more and more of the Messiah as we press ourselves against the new interior landscapes.

*

When their interiors are examined, it is found that the cells are topologically complex structures. They are in motion. They are neither liquid nor crystal but have the properties of both. The organelles and the ultramicroscopic surfaces are in motion both morphologically and chemically. Some of these reproduce, create new substances by chemical combination, or transmit codes for activity. Meat is the only known negentropic system. We can move to the level of the gene within the nucleus of the cell and find long molecules comprised of thousands of submolecules. These threadlike molecules are double helixes—they mirror themselves. The spiral double-thread, which is of extraordinary length and thinness compared to other molecules, has compressed, or encapsuled, or shaped itself into a compact bundle. The genes (which are the memory of the meat plasm) are comprised of atoms of normal and abundant elements.

These atoms come from the earth. We are sure that there was once no life and there has come into being more and more over billionic years. The planet surface becomes complexly arranged by changing into life. The energy trapped in the complex structures is the energy of the sun's rays as they touch the living and becoming-living surface of the earth. The trapped energy begins in simple plants and is passed up a food chain.

There is no clear demarcation of where these complex molecules cease being inert and come to be *life*. It is clear that under certain circumstances the self-formation of these life molecules is a natural phenomenon. ((Scientists have suggested that there may be trigger mechanisms that drift through space, land on planetary surfaces, and bring the or-

ganic into being. Perhaps
somewhere on some other sur-
face, though chances might be
quintillionically against it, there
are moas, giant ground sloths,
glyptodons, Carolina parakeets,
passenger pigeons, steller's sea
cows, or other creatures that we
have destroyed in our primate
blaze.))

*

We know little about MATTER—and it would be better to say
"MATTERS." A verbal progression can be expressed: CREA-
TURE / CELL / CELL INTERIOR / GENE / PLANET SURFACE
/ PLANET / SUN AND SOLAR SYSTEM / GALAXY / UNI-
VERSE / UNIVERSES. One single being! It is impossible to
imagine that this being is limited by the rules that our meat
experiences as time, space, objective reality. We can assume
that we view only the matter origin of our bodies and that
there are other matters and relationships extending in un-
known manners and invisibly linking them with the totality.

Sperms dance with the egg within a fluid, spinning the egg
with their tails till a single sperm capsule attaches itself to the
surface of the egg and extrudes its halved gene material into
the halved gene material of the egg. Then a unique confluence
of events takes place—a creature is united in its first streaming.
With the specific genetic information is created a wolf, a Mo-
zart, a mouse, or a penguin, from the vast propensities of the
single plasmic expanding being. The creature moves on the
surface frontier of the earth, looks out into the universe and
says, "MEAT IS SPIRIT. I FEEL IT. I AM IT. I TOUCH IT. I SEE
IT. I PERCEIVE WITH THE SENSES I AM GIVEN IN THE

POSSIBILITY OF THE SURGE. I CONSTELLATE AND RE-CONSTELLATE THE INFORMATION I AM GIVEN. I MOVE. I AM. I BE. I MAY EVEN ENVISION THE WHIRLING GYRE OF MILLIONIC STARS THAT VAGUELY RESEMBLES THE HELIX DIRECTING MY CELLS."

IV.
A MAMMAL GALLERY

THE GIANT PANDA, huge mammal, furred in black and white, basks and lolls in the shadiness of the bamboo grove. The panda sometimes sits like a man, on his rump with legs outspread, on an earthy mound covered with moss. Perhaps he looks at his beloved and family. He is surrounded by his nutriment, by the tips of bamboo plants that reach many times his height from the surface of the earth towards the sun. Perhaps strange, thoughtless philosophies drift across the platens of his sensorium and create and recreate themselves in his limbs and organs. All of his being is an accumulation of his plasm and the activities of his body. He sprang from the matter of the earth as it was energied by the nearby star that he sees through the sparse places in the glade.

The bamboos about the panda are air creatures. They draw nitrates, some material substance, and water from the earth through the pores of their searching motile root tips. But much of the substance of the bamboo is drawn from thin air, from the gasses of the atmosphere, which are changed by a chemical cycle and the sun's rays into solid substance. Gasses become the BODY of the panda via the bamboo. The bamboos are threads that reach from the planet toward the star that energies them.

AN INVISIBLE WATCHER is in a room with a man and woman who are arguing—they are a lover and beloved, a man and wife. They are quarrelling about the payment on a car, or about the loss of a laundry ticket. The argument becomes too intensive for so minor an issue. It appears that the man and woman are enacting a rite. If the invisible observer closes his ears to the *meanings* of the words and listens only to the vocalization as *sounds,* a thought occurs to him:

He is listening to two mammals. It might be two snow leopards, two bison, two wolves. It is a *mammal* conversation. The man and woman are growling, hissing, whimpering, cooing, pleading, cajoling, and threatening. The specific rite and biomelodic patterning of meat conversation rises and falls in volume. It makes variations, it repeats itself, it begins again, it grows, diminishes. There is a hiss and counterhiss. There is a reply and new outburst. The game that the man and woman are enacting, and the ritual, is as old as their plasm. It is capable of extremes of nervous modulation because of their neuronic complexity but it is more than ancient—it is an Ur-rite.

If the man and woman are lucky, and if their intelligences are open, then one of them will HEAR that it is a rite—that they are growling and hissing. Then he, or she, will laugh at the comedy and the ridiculousness of the pretext. The other partner will laugh in response, intuiting the same perception. Most likely it is a sexual ritual. They are hungry for contact with each other. Their intellective and emotional processes have been frozen into simulations of indifference by pressures of the surroundings and events. If they are lucky enough, one of them will raise a hand to the other, and touch or stroke, recognizing the other as the universe, the counterpart of a star, a galaxy, a planet, a bacterium, a virus, a leopard. Then they have enacted and completed a *tantra* of Shiva and Shakti. They have become mammals and gods and goddesses.

A MAN IS SITTING CROSS-LEGGED in bright afternoon sun-
light. He opens a book of reproductions of Egyptian art. Clear
light gleams off the paper. The *alto relievo* statuary is uncanny.
The lazy intellectual mind scans the opposite page and finds
text describing the statuary in a foreign language. It says, ap-
parently, that this is a Pharaoh and two goddesses. The man's
attention returns to the reproduction—a passing perception
takes the shape of a fragmentary poem:

THE MESSENGER (RNA)
slides to the ribosome
(to the Constellation).
The beads move.
The Pharaoh, Chacal, & Hathor
are glabrous
perfectly
balanced
arm in arm. The weight
of the Man-God
is on
one foot / or the other.
They create the gleam
of this dimension,
of this single
process,
of perfection.
But who is who? and WHAT?

The words mime the balance of the figures as they stand—
Goddess, Pharaoh, Goddess—side by side, touching one an-
other. Their weight is immaculately balanced. The sculptor of
the archaic figures had a knowledge difficult to regain, though
easy to reperceive thousands of years later.

The sculptor sensed that man-mammal is created from the inside outward. That man begins at the interior of his cells and from their perfect balance the body is created.

((Within the human body the RNA slides through the walls of the cell's nucleus, through infinitesimal tubes in the structure, and finds the pearllike ribosome bodies in the cytoplasm. The bodies MOVE *across* the long threadlike molecules of RNA and create the substances of the cell.))

The three figures show muscular development that is excellent, generalized, not excessive. The bodies rest naturally in mammal fashion. A wolf can be seen standing in relaxation, peering with interest, involved and yet disinvolved. The carved stone reproduces muscle tone that is healthy and without contradictory strains. The faces of the Pharaoh and goddesses are as interesting, or as uninteresting, as the faces of snow leopards. Their bodies are erect, with the pelvis slightly forward to balance the weight of the head. The Pharaoh stands with one foot a little forward—it is impossible to tell which foot bears his weight, or if both feet do. The goddesses stand in variations of this posture.

I STAND IN FRONT of the cyclone wire cage containing the female snow leopard. My friend has a tape recorder. We have been taping sounds of animals before the zoo opens. I step over the guardrail where the snow leopardess is watching us. She is indifferent to humans when they keep at a distance. Her task is to fight the physical psychosis of encagement and madness. Most of her waking is spent pacing the constricted outlines of her cage. But now it is early morning and she is resting. When I step over the guard rail she growls in anger without moving— except her head, which swivels to watch me.

No part of her can reach through the mesh of the cyclone wire. I put my face almost to the wire and nearly to her face. There are only a few inches between her mouth and my face. She is enraged, and her face, which seems divine in such proximity, twists into feline lines of rage. The anger and rage are clearer than the conflicting human expressions on the daily streets. She knows the uselessness of pawing or clawing at me.

She puts her face within an inch of the wire and SPEAKS to me. The growl begins instantly and almost without musical attack. It begins gutturally. It grows in volume and it expands till I can feel the interior of her body from whence the energy of the growl extends itself as it gains full volume of fury. It extends itself, vibrating and looping. Then, still with the full capacity of untapped energy, the growl drops in volume and changes in pitch to a hiss. The flecks of her saliva spatter my face. I feel not smirched but cleansed. Her eyes are fixed on me. The growl, without a freshly drawn breath, begins again. It is a language that I understand more clearly than any other. I hear rage, anger, anguish, warning, pain, even humor, fury— all bound into one statement.

I am surrounded by the physicality of her speech. It is a real thing in the air. It absorbs me and I can hear and feel and see nothing else. Her face and features disappear, becoming one entity with her speech. The speech is the purest, most perfect music I have ever heard, and I know that I am touched by the divine, on my cheeks, and on my brow, and on the tympanums of my ears, and the vibrations on my chest, and on the inner organs of perception.

It is music-speech. It is like the music one hears when he places his head on the stomach of his beloved. The gurglings, the drips, the rumblings, the heart, and the pulsebeats in the interior of the body are perfect music. It is the meat speaking and moving—as the testicles move and twist and writhe within the sac making their own motility and pursuing their ends. I am overcome with the universality of the experience. I hope that the drops of leopard saliva will never dry on my face.

We play back the several minutes of this growl and it is more beautiful than any composition of Mozart. Three-quarters of the way into the tape is the clear piercing crow of a bantam rooster making his reply to the *mise-en-scène* about him—to the calls of his ladies, to the sparrows, to the sounds of traffic, to the growling of the leopardess, to the morning sun, to the needs of his own being to vocally establish his territory. The crow of the tiny rooster is smaller but no less perfect or monumental or meaningful than the statement of the leopardess—they make a gestalt. The tape is a work of art as we listen. But we have no desire to add it to the universe of media and plastic artifacts. We see, hear, feel through the veil. WE are translated.

TRAVELLING ON A SMALL SHIP to the Farallon Islands near the San Francisco coast, I spoke with a virologist who had just returned from Australia. He was travelling to the Farallons to study the rabbits there. A lighthouse keeper's son had a pair of rabbits that escaped on the island. The rabbits and their progeny devastated the island of every leaf of plant life. The island was left bare rock, without any vestige of higher plant life. The virologist believed that the rabbits—still populous on the island—ate the desiccated corpses of gulls and seabirds. His idea was that only one type of rabbit had the capability of surviving under these conditions.

I wandered on the island—seeing a rabbit and traces of rabbits—but not a blade of grass or a bush. The island is rocky, craggy, like a miniature, eroding crest of the Alps. After climbing the tiny peak, I descended to the beach, which was scattered with boulderlike rocks. I found myself looking down onto a herd of sea lions, the closest no more than thirty feet away. They were drowsing and lolling in the sun. Seeing something comic in the scene, I raised my hand and began speaking as if I were delivering a sermon. The astonished sea lions dived into the ocean. The ones in the ocean swung about to see me. They began a chorus of YOWPS, and huge angered MEAT CRIES, dense in volume and range. I continued my performance and they carried on their yowping. Perhaps thirty or forty of the animals were yowling at one time. They were FURIOUS, ENRAGED, ASTONISHED. Like the leopardess, their voices were driven by hundreds of pounds of meat force and energy. I was frightened, worried that they might change about, clamber out, and pursue me. They remained in the water cursing me in a clear ancient language that left little doubt about meaning.

AND THEN I knew that not only were the monster shapes of meat enraged, they were PLEASED. THEY WERE SMILING

AS WELL AS ENRAGED! They were overjoyed to be stimulated to anger by a novel—and clearly harmless—intruder. Undoubtedly they enjoyed my astonishment and fear as well as the physical pleasure of their rage. Perhaps they relished my physical reaction to their blitzkrieg of sound. They began to yowp not only at me but to each other.

My ears could not take it any longer and I began walking up the beach. I walked halfway around the island. Five members of the tribe followed in the waves. They watched, taunted, encouraged, scolded, and enjoyed me to the fullest. I have not been in finer company.

CAN THE HUMAN TYPE know more mammal experience, universe perception, and possibilities of joy, or of the cherubic? The music of the body is as lovely as Mozart. Hail Saint Rimbaud! Hail Saint Jesus! Hail Saint Raphael! Hail Muhammad Ali! Hail Sainted painters of the Sung Dynasty! Hail Saint Francis Crick! Give me your gift, but do NOT *intercede* for me with a messiah that YOU visualize. Within me is the UNIVERSE—and outside too. We are extrusions, facets, auras, in vibratory flowing surge of infinite possibilities.

I AM A MAN AND I AM A MAMMAL!
—I
KNOW
I AM.

Part Three

HAIL THEE WHO PLAY!

OH MUSE,

SING THAT I BE ME, BE THOU,

BE MEAT,

be me, be I, no ruse
—A MAMMALED MAN,
and stand
with rainbow robes
that drop away and globes
that float in air about my hand.
A UNIVERSE IN FIGURE EIGHTS
swirls about my head
in flashing neon-lighted dots and blurs and spots
and heavy lines of triumph energy
that lie within my skin.
I raise this knife, this wand, with blade
so thin . . .
I lie upon a circled, polished table
AND LEAP UP
to be myself again ! ! ! ! !

! OH POTENCY !
To be my self-soiled soul,

SPIRIT AGAIN,

AND NOTHING MORE !

I AM MY ABSTRACT ALCHEMIST OF FLESH
made real!
I AM MY ABSTRACT ALCHEMIST OF FLESH
made real!
I AM MY ABSTRACT ALCHEMIST OF FLESH
made real!
And nothing more!
NO LESS THAN STAR—
a chamber and a vacuole.
Without sense!   A Thing!   I feel!

I am not gold nor steel!
I am not metal, sulfur, nor the flow of Mercury!!!!
I am not the berry crumbling in my cheek
with rasping seeds that speak
of summer sun, or salmon in the creek
that stretch themselves, writhing
on the pebbled beach to catch the gasp of twilight
IN THE CAVERN OF THEIR MIGHT

and feel the sunbeam crash the slime

AND CATCH THE GLINT.

I'M SHEERLY ARM AND LEG
that bounces from the slashing beam
of heat
AND NOTHING MORE!!!!!!
!OH MUSE!
!OH ME!

THIS IS THE CUPID'S FACE with Eros grin;
these are the cheeks that make the mask
so thin.
These eyes are holes within the sight of what's within.
I laugh, I weep, I break the task
that roils and flashes in the flask
like a sinking sailing ship
or statue in the lighted night
ABOUT ME!!!

THIS IS MY MEAT!
A flaming fur of skin!
My chin's an axe,
a snapping whip,
a gentle thing
like moths and wax
that glimmer in the white
about my light!

NECK IS A COLUMN OF MY MEAT.
I gleam at thee
—a shambling, hulking bulk that will not skulk
in cowardice or terror
in the fingers, feathers, leaves, or steel.
I AM MY ABSTRACT ALCHEMIST OF FLESH
MADE REAL!

I AM THE SILHOUETTE THAT MOVES IN BLACK,
a profile making the attack
on space and growing to be the meat
that moves within . . .
BUT I AM OUT, WITHIN THE VALE WHERE SOULS
are made.
My brain is struck again
by eyes that window on the world
that leads into the stars, and nebulae, and swirls
that sink into the matter's heart.

AND I AM LIGHT ! ! ! !

I AM A CAVE

I

ACT
WITHIN ! ! ! !

I AM THE CENSOR WHERE THE SMOKE OF PERFUME
MAKES MY DREAMS.
I am the melody that screams
for silence on the boom
that guides the prow.
I am the tracery of wind that blows
the sail
and also creatures sleeping on the veldt.
I SEE *ALL THINGS* ARE MEN !

THE TORTURERS THAT BURN THE BABES
ARE NEITHER BLACK NOR WHITE
but Men!
They will put on their rainbow robes again!
The horrors in the night are real!

I AM A ROSE!!!!

ALL SPACE WILL TWIST ITSELF TO SHAPES OF MEAT

and I am FREE!
IMAGINATION GIVES ME WHAT I AM!!!!
A woman's picture burns itself within my head
—I raise my skirts
of velvet, silk, or lace, or lead.
There are no hurts
EXCEPT THE PAINS MADE REAL!
They act in trillionic clouds of stars
to create themselves among the bodies
of their slain.
They are naked injured dragons in their planes
and concrete rooms with movies on the walls
forgetting they are mammal men!

THE PITS BENEATH MY EYES
ARE HOLLOWS IN
THE NIGHT WHERE SERAPHS DWELL.
The things I brutalize are less
than Hell.
I torture flesh and I caress the zones
where youth still swells.
BUT SEE THESE MAMMAL MEN
and listen to their knell
that counterpoints upon a billion screens
(and echoes each vibration
each sensation
in ecstasies of twisted hands). Scenes
line behind each other past
infinity. OH,
BLESS
their aches and pains and kill them well!!!!!!!
Let them return and never spurn
the elves and worms they walk upon.

STOP THE ONES WHO KILL WITHOUT THEIR
PRIDE'S COMMAND!

I see *ALL THINGS* are men!

THE LION AND THE LIONESS THAT
SLEEP UPON THE VELDT
am I.
The brocade curtains on my sight
draw back and watch the fly
that moves upon the ochre grass.
—I hear him speak.
No manly being is too weak
to be a mass
the size of nebulae.
The cliffs are profiles quick
to move.
Leviathonic shapes
which laughter quakes
are tiny grapes
beneath my microscope.
THE SKY IS FLOOR I SLEEP UPON.
God and Goddess knock upon my door.
THE GOD IS HERE
in drunken revel
hanging in the air!

!OH NO!

The bat and vision circle round
the fingertip
I touch to lip
—or anywhere—in my lair.

OH DO NOT KILL!
BLESS
those who love you still
OR QUICK.
The MASS of things are sick
when seen with rotten eyes;
THE STIES
of Paradiso are filled with Cherubim.

The moon shines on blackness
far beneath
and speeds with me.
I am a MAN!
I am a tree!
The Moon above holds
out its hands
in radiant beams.
I live and fight in streams
of blasting Joy and Hate.
Bless the God who worships me!

THE JUNCTURE IS THE PAST MADE REAL !
THE HEART'S A NET
to search within with chromium stylet.
!!!!!OH NO!!!!!
OH NO!!!   OH NO!!!
The Blackness is a bet
that's made between the gods and demonkind.
The absence of all things is merely spirit
set within a hole in nowhere
beckoning me. There is no fear
of where to be.
Silhouettes of angels move within my meaty palm.
THERE IS NO WET
nor dry
except in places where
I touch upon.
THIS IS THE NIGHT TURNED SNOWY DAY
with crystals on the lip and tip
of tongue
and we are dreamers pressed against a window pane.

!!!OH NO—OH YES!!!

HAIL thee who play.

!HAIL THEE WHO PLAY!

Reading List

Ashvaghosha. *The Awakening of Faith.* Edited by Alan Hull Walton. Translated by Timothy Richard. London: Charles Skilton, 1961.

Artaud, Antonin. *Selected Writings of Artaud.* Edited by Susan Sontag. Translated by Helen Weaver. New York: Farrar, Straus & Giroux, 1976.

Blackburn, Paul. *Early Selected y Mas: Poems, 1949–1966.* Los Angeles: Black Sparrow, 1972.

Blake, William. *The Poetry and Prose of William Blake.* Edited by Geoffrey Keynes. London: Nonesuch, 1927.

Chang, Garma C. C. *The Buddhist Teaching of Totality: The Philosophy of Hwa Yen Buddhism.* University Park, PA: Pennsylvania State University Press, 1971.

Crane, Hart. *Collected Poems of Hart Crane.* Edited by Waldo Frank. New York: Liveright, 1933.

Creeley, Robert. *Later.* New York: New Directions, 1979.

Crick, Francis. *Of Molecules and Men.* Seattle: University of Washington Press, 1967.

Dante Alighieri. *The Divine Comedy.* Translated by Lawrence Grant White. Pantheon: New York, 1948.

Duncan, Robert. *Letters.* Highlands, NC: Jonathan Williams, 1958.

Ginsberg, Allen. *"Howl" and Other Poems.* San Francisco: City Lights, 1956.

Haeckel, Ernst. *The Riddle of the Universe at the Close of the Nine-*

teenth Century. Translated by Joseph McCabe. New York: Harper and Brothers, 1900.

Herakleitos and Diogenes. *Herakleitos of Ephesius and Diogenes the Cynic.* Translated by Guy Davenport. San Francisco: Grey Fox, 1979.

Jerison, Harry J. *Evolution of the Brain and Intelligence.* New York: Academic Press, 1973.

Keleman, Stanley, *Somatic Reality.* Berkeley: Center Press, 1979.

Kerouac, Jack. *Mexico City Blues.* New York: Grove, 1959.

Lawrence, D. H. *Complete Poems.* Edited by Vivian de Sola Pinto and Warren Roberts. New York: Viking, 1964.

Manyōshū. *Manyōshū: The Nippon Gakujutsu Translation of One Thousand Poems.* New York: Columbia University Press, 1969.

Margalef, Ramon. *Perspectives in Ecological Theory.* Chicago: University of Chicago Press, 1968.

Margulis, Lynn. *Origin of the Eukaryotic Cells.* New Haven: Yale University Press, 1970.

Martin, P. S. and H. E. Wright. *Pleistocene Extinctions: The Search for a Cause.* New Haven: Yale University Press, 1968.

Morowitz, Harold J. *Energy Flow in Biology.* New York: Academic Press, 1968.

Odum, Howard T. *Environment, Power, and Society.* New York: Wiley-Interscience, 1971.

Olson, Charles. *The Maximus Poems, Volume Three.* Edited by Charles Boer and George F. Butterick. New York: Grossman, 1975.

———*Selected Writings.* Edited by Robert Creeley. New York: New Directions, 1967.

Sahlins, Marshall. *Stone Age Economics.* Chicago: Aldine-Atherton, 1972.

Shelley, P. B. *Complete Poetical Works.* Edited by Neville Rogers. Oxford: Clarendon, 1972.

Snyder, Gary. *The Back Country.* New York: New Directions, 1968.

Tobias, Philip V. *The Brain in Hominid Evolution.* New York: Columbia University Press, 1971.

Whalen, Philip. *Like I Say.* New York: Totem/Corinth, 1960.

Whitehead, Alfred North. *The Function of Reason.* Boston: Beacon, 1958.

Yip, Wai-Lim. *Chinese Poetry: Major Modes and Genres.* Berkeley: University of California Press, 1976.

Design by David Bullen
Typeset in Mergenthaler Sabon
by Robert Sibley
Printed by Maple-Vail
on acid-free paper